BAREFOOT
BALANCHINE

ANCHOR

BOOKS

NEW YORK

LONDON

TORONTO

SYDNEY

AUCKLAND

BAREFOOT TO BALANCHINE

How to Watch Dance

MARY KERNER

FOREWORD BY RUTH PAGE

ILLUSTRATIONS BY DELPHINE LOUIE

AN ANCHOR BOOK

PUBLISHED BY DOUBLEDAY

a division of Bantam Doubleday Dell Publishing Group, Inc.
666 Fifth Avenue, New York, New York 10103

ANCHOR BOOKS, DOUBLEDAY, and the portrayal of an anchor
are trademarks of Doubleday, a division of Bantam Doubleday
Dell Publishing Group, Inc.

BOOK DESIGN BY BARBARA M. BACHMAN
TITLE PAGE ILLUSTRATION BY DELPHINE LOUIE

Library of Congress Cataloging-in-Publication Data
Kerner, Mary.
Barefoot to Balanchine : how to watch dance / by Mary
Kerner.—1st ed.
p. cm.
Includes bibliographical references.
1. Dancing. 2. Dancing—History. 3. Dancing—
Terminology. 4. Modern dance. 5. Modern dance—
History. I. Title.
GV1594.K47 1990
792.8—dc20   90-662
CIP

ISBN 0-385-26436-4

To
Miss Tania
Mr. B
&
Terpsichore

Making her stage debut at the age of eight, **Mary Kerner** began dance training with Tatiana Dokoudovska of the original Ballet Russe, followed by professional work with Ruth Page's Chicago Opera Ballet and modern dance pioneer Hanya Holm. She has taught technique, appreciation, criticism, and writing at universities (including her alma mater, Smith College), and has worked with Merce Cunningham's dance company in public relations and publicity. She now interviews and writes extensively, and has been published in the *Christian Science Monitor*, *Ballet News*, *Ballet Review*, *Dance Magazine*, *Dance Teacher Now*, the *Chicago Tribune*, the *Los Angeles Times*, and Reuters international wire.

She lives near the ocean on a ranch in Marin County, California, with her sheltie named Balanchine.

ACKNOWLEDGMENTS

This book owes its nascence to Tania Dokoudovska, who introduced me to the onstage how-to, and Richard Dryden, who continued my education in the backstage wherefore; and all the performers and companies who ever gave me joy.

In addition, the author wishes to thank the following people for their kind support, advice, and assistance: Gerald Arpino, Rosalind DeMille, David Vaughan, Geri Stuparich, Jane Sheeks, Robert Gottlieb, William Van Voris, Sally Streets, Mary Morris, Jason Klein, Peter Stelzer and Marla Frumkin, Joy Bowman, Renee Renouf, Paul Parish, Carl Wilson, the Wylands, Center for the Arts, Martin David, Cynthia Gwin, Montalvo, and my dear editors at the *Monitor*—Alan Bunce, Fred Guidry, Bruce Manual.

Special thanks go to:

Dick Boehm, who kept me from throwing in the towel at the end; and Carolyn Reidy, who had the foresight to see what I envisioned at the beginning.

My patient editor, Sallye Leventhal, who—always cheerfully—brought this project to fruition.

And, last but never least, the one who listened and missed sleep, listened and encouraged, listened and comforted. For the best critic's critic ever, all my love.

CONTENTS

A P P E N D I C E S

FOREWORD

Dancers are a breed apart. Although it sometimes seems that all their knowledge is in their feet, it is their brains that rule their feet.

My whole life has been devoted to dance: I can't dance anymore, which puts me in a position where I am on the outside looking in.

There are so many facets to dance, and Mary Kerner successfully describes each one of them in this book. With it as your guide, everything you will see on the stage is illuminated in an entertaining way. How, then, could anyone help but come to love the performances?

Mary Kerner's book is refreshing and spontaneous; like dancing itself, she has made a grand effort, which is marvelous for dance audiences.

I still adore dance, and I think everyone else will too, especially after reading this fascinating book.

Ruth Page

AUTHOR'S

INTRODUCTION

The genesis of this book was a comment I've heard far too often from dance-goers: "I thought it was good, but then what do I know?" It is my opinion that the average member of the audience knows a great deal about what looks good and what doesn't; about what excites and what doesn't; about what creates the passion that makes dance-going an obsession for some, and about the qualities that make others want to stay at home. Yet for some reason, this same audience feels itself to be uninformed, unenlightened, or out of touch with dance—and thus does dance remain rarefied.

Dance is accessible to everyone—and that means anyone. People danced long before they could talk. Dance is a means of communication, a means of expression that is universal. You don't have to take a technique class to be able to feel the exuberance of the leaping dancer or the sensuality of a man and woman dancing together. But training can help. And I mean training the eye. Your heart has all the information it needs. So do your muscles: they respond kinesthetically to watching movement.

It amuses me that audience members feel themselves ill-equipped to discuss a performance but they never question the authority of a critic. Where do critics get this power with which audiences vest them? If a critic has anything over an audience member, it might be the experience of watching dance more often. This still doesn't mean they necessarily know more, only that they will have learned to recognize the elements that separate good performances from bad. Beyond that, a lot of what they write is personal opinion. I believe that a person can be taught *how* to watch dance but not *what* to enjoy. That's your decision, not a critic's.

The purpose of dance criticism is to serve the audience— to educate, to inform, and, especially, to preserve an eva- nescent art form. Even in this age of television and videotape, there is nothing quite like attending a live performance. The closest to capturing it for those who weren't there is the prose of the critic . . . or the educated descriptions of the informed audience member. A critic's review should give you the feeling of what the performance looked—and, more important, felt —like. It should tell you something about the company, the dancer, the choreography, and the performance. In other words, you should know about dancing when you finish reading.

What I am suggesting is the possible heresy that being a critic is not just a matter of having a staff position on a major publication, complimentary tickets on the aisle, and the right to say anything in a review. Audiences are also critics. Whether an audience is enjoying the performance or not can be felt by the dancers onstage. And how audience members react to a certain performance will—and should—determine whether they buy a ticket to another performance by that company or that dancer. If you're sitting in the audience and you aren't asleep, you are watching with a critical eye—whether you know it or not.

This book is about how to be your own critic. You don't have to rely on anyone else's opinion; you don't have to ask whether a performance was good or not; and, after reading this book, you won't wonder when to buy a ticket. You'll know how to watch dance—which includes what to expect, why performances look the way they do, which steps are most difficult, and what went into getting the dance onstage.

The rest is up to you. Your body and your heart, not your mind, are going to tell you what you liked. And that's what dance watching is about—loving something so much you'll go back again and again and again.

Before getting into the specifics of how to watch, there are a few points which should be made clear. Most important is my intention that the distinction between ballet and modern dance be minimalized. Over the years, the separation between these two forms of dance has decreased so as to make them almost indiscernible. Ballet companies perform modern or contemporary choreography, and modern dance choreographers create ballets.

Except where a distinction applies, the text refers to dance as a whole. To me, dance is ballet, modern, jazz, Broadway, ethnic, and ballroom—whatever movement is performed onstage for an audience. Also, I use the term BALLET in its generic sense as a *dance*, such as "going to the ballet," which means attending a dance performance. Whether ballet or modern choreography, the terms PIECE, DANCE, and BALLET are used interchangeably to refer to a performance selection.

Also, throughout the text when I refer to either a male or female dancer, I use the terms DANSEUR and BALLERINA, respectively. Originally variations of these titles were used to designate rank at the Paris Opéra (such as *premier* danseur and *prima* ballerina). In American ballet companies, most of this hierarchy has been eliminated—except the designation of corps, soloists, and principals, which are modified slightly from company to company. Therefore, I use danseur and ballerina to refer to male and female dancers, whether referring to stars or not, for the sake of simplicity.

Finally, specific dancers are mentioned in this book for illustrative purposes. They may not necessarily be seen onstage now or in the future, but their dancing, or their stories, are useful for the viewer in the context of this book. No attempt has been made to include everyone the knowledgeable dance-goer should know, or even everyone who has made an important contribution to the field of dance. The purpose of their inclusion, like the rest of this book, is to enhance your viewing of dance.

For those of you who already have a working knowledge of some of the topics mentioned in this book—technique, steps, history, or criticism—please note that many aspects have been simplified, and not everything possible included, in order to maintain the focus of the book, which is enjoying performance from an audience standpoint.

(The Suggested Reading in the appendices is intended to carry the interested reader more deeply into the subjects mentioned herein.)

BAREFOOT TO BALANCHINE

PART ONE

HOW TO WATCH

DANCE

How to watch dance has to do with what you *can expect*, not what you *should enjoy*. Kinesthetic awareness is probably the most important tool of the dance watcher. In other words, if you don't know how to *watch* dance, try "feeling" it.

Everyone has kinesthetic awareness, or the ability to feel muscular sympathy without actually doing the movement. For instance, when the audience gasps as a dancer leaps high, they are responding verbally to what is visual. Taken one step further, an audience can also respond *in* their bodies, or feel what the dancer is doing. Probably everyone, in response to some performance, has experienced that urge to assist one dancer lift another into the air or to help a dancer balance—that is kinesthetic awareness.

What you are looking for when you watch dance is that response—the feeling that you are dancing along with the performers, and a sense that dancing is effortless, as if you might go home and do it yourself. You are looking for expressive freedom, physical lightness, and that indefinable quality called grace. These intangibles should be felt—in your muscles, not just in your mind.

In other words, what you are looking for is quality, and that quality, in the visceral art that is dance, may more often be felt than seen. Quality has to do with the subtle difference between what is merely professional and what is truly great. The great dancer takes your breath away; the adequate professional has you talking about what he or she did. Technique is easier to analyze than the qualities that pushed a performance *beyond* good into great. The better the performance, the more difficult it is to evaluate.

Dancing is not just the steps put together accurately. Steps do contribute to the dancing, and the more you know about them, the more you will appreciate what constitutes good dancing. But technique is not performance. Quality has to do with security, ease, confidence, and bravura, all giving an edge of élan to a performance. These elements may not be technique per se. They might better be categorized as style, or a manner that presents dancing as easy, performing as fun. The higher the performance level of the dancers, the lower the anxiety level of the audience. Performances are more exciting when the dancers are so secure they can add an element of risk to what they do; when the attack is bold and sure; when the audience gasps with joy, not relief.

This quality includes a special musicality, a dancing "on" or with the beat. Some dancers are lovely, but they have no discernible sense of rhythm that allows them to dance as if enhancing the music, not just mechanically going through the steps. The same goes for emotion behind the technique. Does that dancer make you love the movement or just watch it?

Beyond these elusive aspects of quality that involve more feeling than seeing, there are specifics to watch for, some of a technical nature, forming the base from which a dancer can then go "beyond technique."

Among those easiest to spot onstage are the number of **turns** a dancer makes and how those turns are brought to a complete stop. The more turns, the harder they are to execute properly. Due to the buildup of momentum, a dancer may either have difficulty staying in one place or trouble stopping the turns steadily. The completion is all-important—for different turns there are specific end poses, which should be executed without hesitation, or going off balance. For example, when the ballerina finishes a series of turns she should come to a dead halt—no extra little steps, or "adjusting," as it is called in the trade.

The landing position varies, but is generally on one foot with the other out behind, either with the extended toe pointed on the floor, or in the air in *arabesque* (one leg extended behind). A more difficult variation of a landing position would be on *half pointe* (on the ball of the foot), or *sur les pointes* (on the tips of the toes) for the ballerina. The same requirements apply to the male dancer, or *danseur*, whether he is completing turns in place or those that circle the stage. His body should stop revolving as if he'd put on the brakes, again without jerking, wobble, or hesitation.

Speed is another consideration. Faster is generally more difficult in dance, though at times, certain turns and leaps are easier to execute when speed aids momentum. Speed is also to be applauded when it involves intricate footwork. Practice and careful training are required to get many steps done in a short time. Steps which are relatively simple at one tempo become difficult when performed at another. A famous example is a series of *retirés* (placing the toes of the working foot against the knee of the supporting leg) by the solo ballerina in *Raymonda*. She begins them very slowly, gradually building up speed, until the last few are done at a lightning pace. While the *retiré* is a relatively simple and rudimentary move, getting the foot up to the knee and back down to the floor quickly —and perfectly—is not.

Going on and off *pointe* quickly is also quite difficult. In other words, a *triple pirouette sur les pointes* (or three turns on the toes in the same place), is easier than three *fouettés* (or turns in which the working leg "whips" out to the side after each revolution). The *pirouette* is done completely on *pointe*, while the *fouetté* requires coming down off *pointe* between each revolution. The effort of flattening and then pointing the foot makes the *fouetté* harder than the *pirouette* done totally on *pointe*.

Direction is also a factor in assessing technique. Turns performed in a circle are much harder than those done in a straight line across the stage. Having to stay in one place, as opposed to "traveling," while turning, is tricky as well. Watch the ballerina doing *fouettés* or the male *danseur* doing turns *à la seconde* to see that the supporting foot stays in the same place. A tilt of the arms, shoulders, or upper torso suggests that the dancer is leaning off-balance. If one shoulder is dropped, the body will start moving in that direction. And if one arm is lower than the other, or drags behind the other, the body will also waver off-center. Ideally, all turns done "in place" should begin and end with the feet in exactly the same spot on the stage.

Changing direction while turning or leaping requires mastery of "spotting." This term refers to keeping the head still while the body rotates, whipping the head around at the last second, and focusing the eyes on a spot in the distance. If the point of focus changes frequently, which it will for turns in a circle, the dancer must have better balance and control.

Changing arms or legs while turning or leaping is another challenge. *Piqué* or *chaîné* turns, both of which are the "traveling" variety, are those most likely to exhibit arm changes. For instance, the top arm in fifth position overhead may switch to fifth position *en bas* (low), while the opposite arm goes to fifth *en haut* (above). The arms may thus reverse on each turn, adding to the possible factors that might throw the dancer off-balance.

When it comes to leaps, balance is equally important. In addition to stopping still, a **quiet landing** after a leap should be on the critical checklist. Control is often the key to dance technique. A dancer who comes crashing down from a leap cancels out the beauty of *en l'air* maneuvers.

The **height of a leap** certainly adds to one's enjoyment of dance. It is the spectacular and continual overcoming of gravity that makes the athleticism of dance so challenging. But this quality is not nearly so important as that of **sustaining**. The airborne dancer should look, if only for a fraction of a second, to be pausing midair. This illusion is one of the grandest of the dance—that additional second when the body unfolds just a little more, the legs stretch out a little longer, and the arms float a little higher. At this crest of the leap is when the dancer seems most to defy nature.

Straight knees are another aspect of technique to look for which are absolutely de rigueur almost any time either leg is extended and most of the time the feet are flat on the floor —except when they are specifically choreographed to be either in *plié* or in *attitude* (leg bent and up in the air). Bent knees can be a sign of laziness, lack of concentration, or an inability to keep up with the tempo. Going from *plié* to straight leg during very fast steps or leaps is quite difficult—sometimes the muscles of the legs don't move as fast as the music.

Pointed toes are a basic requirement of good dance technique, except when modern dance specifically choreographs for the flexed foot. As with straight knees, this is second nature to the professional but difficult to attain when the dancer is doing very quick jumps, as when going on and off the floor at terrific tempos, or in the middle of a series of leaps when the mind is concentrating on getting the body up in the air.

Sometimes one dancer may not appear to have the toes pointed as much as other dancers. This may not be due to sloppiness but to differences in foot structure. The dancer with a stronger metatarsal arch (the one under the ball of the foot) can create a greater arc when the toes are pointed.

In addition to straight knees and pointed toes, dancers are applauded for the height of their legs when in **extension**—or when one leg is stretched away from the body into the air, as in an *arabesque*. Somewhere in the evolution of the dance, extension was considered more important for women, but men can—and do—get their legs up high.

While performing an extension, or any other step that requires one foot to remain stationary, that foot had better do just that—remain still. Wobbling, especially of the ankles, which indicates that the dancer is trying to maintain balance, is not part of the picture. Even though dance may be about bodies moving through space (to paraphrase Merce Cunningham), it is vital that the movement occur only at choreographed moments.

It is wise to bear in mind, in discussions like these, that because dance requires the human body for its medium, it is subject to the imperfections of that instrument. Occasionally, even the finest professional may lose balance, or wobble a bit trying to regain or find it. This may happen one performance in ten or one day in a month, or once in a full-length ballet. Though technically incorrect, it's to be forgiven, if not occasionally expected.

Line is an aspect of dance technique to look for all the time, although it is most obvious in *adagio* movements such as extension. The whole body—head, shoulders, arms, torso, hips and legs—should be in *alignment*. This concept is more difficult to differentiate in modern dance, which often involves body angularity, as opposed to ballet, where the body tends primarily to be elongated. Still, there is always a technically appropriate line inscribed by a body moving through space which has to do with correct carriage. And when it isn't right, you'll intuitively know it. The body will look awkward, spatial dimensions irregular; fluidity is lost when the body cuts space in a broken stage picture.

Partnering—including lifts, supported turns, and balances—should appear effortless, and the **preparation** for each should be unobtrusive. The movement between the two dancers should flow as a natural give-and-take. In the words of Gelsey Kirkland, good partnering is "like conversation."

Partners should also look completely sure of each other. No fear should register on the face of either, nor should there be a tentativeness getting in or out of any pose. Neither should the audience feel any worry about the safety of the dancers, especially when the female is flipped down suddenly from a balanced pose high above the male's head. Great couples are daring with each other. They are not afraid of hurtling themselves toward each other for lifts or dancing with abandon, confident that the other will be exactly where expected when they need to connect. This ease will be palpably apparent to the audience; the lack of it is jarringly evident as well.

Nor should partnering appear to be a great deal of work. Lifts from a stationary position, as when the ballerina is lifted straight off the ground into the air without doing a preparatory run, step, or *plié*, are quite difficult. These require the danseur to lift dead weight—and make it look light. The impression of effortlessness is a matter of timing, technical expertise, and an intuitive sympathy and trust between danseur and ballerina.

In **ensemble work**, such as the *corps de ballet* in *Swan Lake* or unison dancing by all members of a modern dance company, the dancers should be together. Although George Balanchine said no two flowers are alike and therefore no two women's arms are going to be in the same position, it has become standard in classical ballets for the corps to dance as if one, in straight lines, perfect rows, every arm and leg in the same position. Each dancer should be on the beat of the music and dancing as if from the same rhythm of all the other dancers. There should be a smoothness in the interaction between dancers, and a cooperation in which each is sure of where the others are and what they are doing. When true ensemble is seen, the dancers will move from the same impulse, as if performing the same composition on different instruments. There may be individual expression, but the overall picture creates a cohesive whole. In great ensembles, all are secure in their place on the stage and equally sure of the others.

Whether dancing together or separately, dancers should exhibit **smooth recovery**. This suggests more than covering up mistakes gracefully, although that, too, is the sign of a true professional. Recovery refers to coming out of turns to a dead stop, making the transition from leaps to slow steps without adding little adjustments in between, or changing directions with finesse and exactitude. Smooth recovery also can be applied to partnership work, as when coming out of a lift or coming back together for supported *adagio* after doing solos.

Dancers should exude a sense of **confidence**. What is simple and what is difficult technically should be indistinguishable. Ease should characterize everything seen, even if the dancer is actually panting, straining, or struggling because balance is his nemesis, or turning to the left is not her forte.

Not only should it appear effortless, the dancing must seem a pleasure. Within their mastery of execution lies the dancers' ability to enjoy what they are doing. Years of training and the development of a flawless technique evolve into the freedom to dare, to risk, to jump a little higher, turn one more revolution, balance a little longer. Good dancing will take your breath away. The movement will seem so spectacular, while looking so easy, that you'll want to see it again and again.

One critical aspect of good technique defies definition. It is essential that the separate steps, positions, poses, and lifts meld together into something that is more than a mere amalgam of distinct moves. What happens *between* the steps, according to Baryshnikov, is dancing. The rest is only steps strung together. Dancing is more than that—it is also the feelings that go with the execution of those steps. If you have trouble separating the positions you learn in this book from one another when you see performances, then the dancers are doing their job—and more. They are truly dancing.

The following reference checklist outlines all the qualities discussed above. Look for them next time you go to a dance performance.

1. NUMBER OF TURNS, BEATS, LEAPS, ETC.

2. SPEED

3. GOING UP AND DOWN ON AND OFF *POINTE*

4. DIRECTION

5. RECOVERY: STOPPING STILL; QUIET, CONTROLLED LANDINGS

6. HEIGHT OF LEG—EXTENSION

   HEIGHT OF LEAP—ÉLÉVATION

7. SUSTAINING WHEN AIRBORNE

8. BALANCE

9. LINE, ALIGNMENT, PLACEMENT

10. PARTNERING: LIFTS, PRECARIOUS LOOKS SAFE, CONVER-
    SATIONAL FLOW

11. ENSEMBLE: TOGETHER, STRAIGHT LINES

12. MELDING; NO SEPARATION OF STEPS

13. QUALITIES: EASE, CONFIDENCE, BRAVURA, ATTACK,
    FREEDOM, SECURITY

When dancers don't do everything on the checklist exactly right, they may try to compensate by doing what is known in the trade as "cheating." CHEATING is a term used in the dance world for the little adjustments that take place onstage during a performance. For instance, perfect turnout is difficult to achieve when the attention is on getting the leg in *arabesque penchée* as high as perhaps a vertical to the floor. Cheating in this instance would consist of turning in the supporting foot slightly and/or rotating the hip forward.

There are lots of examples of cheating, but none of them is tantamount to cheating the audience. Dancing changes focus and intensity during a performance. Technique class is a time for checking that placement is absolutely accurate. Rehearsal focuses on learning and understanding the choreography, and getting accustomed to spatial relations between dancers.

Performance is for dancing. In performance, adrenaline is up. Concentration is not on steps, on technique, on all those corrections from rehearsal. A performing dancer is thinking only about dancing. If the dancing is very good—the kind that has you on the edge of your seat—the dancer will be letting go, forgetting about particulars, thinking only about the entire body moving through space. In fact, the great dancer, assured of technique and adequately rehearsed, will probably not be thinking at all. The moments of the performance that are most emotionally moving are those in which the dancer is feeling, not thinking.

So while cheating is what most dancers strive to correct during training, onstage it may not be always avoidable. An occasional adjustment, or even cheating, is most likely unintentional. The longer one dances, the more experience one has, and the better the technical assurance, the more a dancer can let go onstage and still be performing every step accurately. When the steps are right, one can forget about them and just dance.

PART TWO

BACKSTAGE:

BEFORE CURTAIN

An air of excitement fills the evening: arriving taxis cause traffic jams, crowds queue impatiently at the doors, ushers bustle up and down the aisles, program notes rustle as they are read, binoculars are pulled out of their cases, musical phrases rise from the orchestra pit. Restlessness.

The lights dim. A spotlight flashes through the darkness, following the conductor. As he steps up on the podium, the audience applauds. He raises his arms for the downbeat. A hush settles over the house.

And then the curtain comes up on another performance of that most evanescent of the arts—dance. Preparation time is over. The audience can just sit back and enjoy the dancing. But what was going on backstage while that same audience was dressing, dining, and arriving?

That morning the dancers took class, for one and a half hours, as they do every day of their lives. That afternoon they rehearsed, anywhere from two to five hours, setting the choreography on that particular stage, running through the pieces to be performed that night, or preparing future repertory.

Sometime between 5 and 6 P.M., the dancers arrived at the theater to warm up. A sign-in sheet on a bulletin board backstage makes sure that everyone needed to dance that evening, or standing by to understudy, is available. If someone doesn't sign in, the company rehearsal assistant, or regisseur, must locate that dancer or find a fill-in. In the case of last-minute illness or injury, this may require quickly running a replacement through his or her paces onstage just before curtain— hence the requirement that every dancer must be signed in by "half-hour," or thirty minutes before curtain.

In the early evening, dancers gave themselves individual *barre* or a set of warm-up exercises to prepare their muscles for the stress their bodies are about to undergo. Proper warm-up is essential so that the muscles aren't strained or injured during the performance. Since dancers must wait backstage between entrances and, of course, between dances, they throw on sweaters and leg warmers over their costumes. The result is rather motley looking: faded leg warmers and baggy sweaters contrast with elegant makeup, elaborate costumes. The purpose of this look, however, is to protect the muscles from the stress of constant starting and stopping, which cause them to heat up and cool down.

But there is more to backstage before a performance than dancers going through their paces at portable *barres* shoved into obscure wings, or stretching on the floor wherever a quiet, nontrammeled spot can be found. In fact, backstage a few hours before a performance is not a particularly quiet place to be.

The **stage manager**, who is king backstage, checks cues and perhaps confers with the orchestra conductor about changes noted at that afternoon's rehearsal. **Stagehands** do their last-minute chores: mopping the stage floor, readjusting lights, checking that curtains and scenery are properly placed. **Costume and prop crew** will be laying out accoutrements on backstage tables or hanging clothes on racks for costume changes. The tremendous orderliness of this procedure makes the dancers, going through their paces alone, appear to be the least important actors in the mini-drama.

After warming up, dancers retire to dressing rooms to put on makeup. The process may be complicated, depending on the role. Dancers sit in front of bright, hot makeup lights. Telegrams are sometimes taped to makeup mirrors. Each dancer brings something personal to his or her makeup table, a good-luck memento or a *merde* gift. (*Merde*, French for "shit," has become a backstage tradition for "Good luck" among dancers, similar to the way actors say "Break a leg" to each other.) Besides whispering *merde* just before going onstage, dancers may exchange *merde* gifts, or tokens that symbolize confidence in a good performance.

Dressers, in large ballet companies, help dancers into the more difficult costumes. Dressers are members of the **wardrobe staff** who repair costumes, paint shoes, help dancers get into costumes before a performance, and are ready backstage to assist with quick changes. For instance, women's tutus and men's jackets are fastened in the back with rows and rows of hooks and eyes or zippers, making them impossible for the dancer to do up alone. Wardrobe will also be spray-painting ballet slippers to match costume colors and sewing alterations in costumes worn by a different dancer for an alternate cast.

This is also a time for contemplation if the role demands a dramatic "persona," or practicing steps onstage one last time. For dancers wearing *pointe* shoes, plenty of time must be allotted to prepare them—a process called BREAKING IN, or working in the shoe until it adheres and responds to the foot.

Meanwhile, the orchestra has arrived. They usually have a separate place from the dancers, such as the "Green Room," to meet, change, and prepare for the stage manager to call them to the pit about five minutes before curtain.

Of the entire cast of backstage characters, the crew appears to be the least agitated by all the activity going on. The company **regisseur** is dashing about, trying to find a corps member. Frantic phone calls, probably from the press representative's backstage office, ensue as a replacement for an injured dancer is tracked down. Flowers are delivered at the stage door. Some are immediately taken to dressing rooms; others are specifically designated for onstage presentation after a dance. The stage manager announces "half hour" thirty minutes before curtain. This is the first warning; other warnings will be "fifteen minutes," "orchestra to the pit," "dancers onstage," and "places."

Boisterousness fades as curtain draws near. Just about the time the greatest influx of audience is arriving and the "house" is at its noisiest, the backstage is approaching its most quiet moment. The company assembles onstage, outer warm-up clothing removed. The orchestra heads for the pit; crewmen take their places at lighting and scenery stations. Dressers stand by with costumes, ready for changes. Onstage, dancers may giggle or whisper nervously; most are jumping, turning, or bobbing up and down—getting into their bodies, feeling their *pointe* shoes, and keeping their muscles warm.

In a split second, the stage manager calls "places," the houselights dim, the applause for the conductor can be heard muffled through the curtain, and—the curtain rises, to either the opening poses of the dancers onstage or their first leaps and bounds of the evening. Looking into the audience, all the dancers see is blinding lights.

But from those lights comes a dancer's favorite music—applause. When to applaud at the ballet has its own tradition, just like the symphony and the opera. Unlike symphony, however, interrupting the action with applause is not only acceptable but encouraged at dance performances.

The most obvious times for applause concern the conductor and the orchestra. Applaud just after the houselights go down when the conductor enters the "pit." This is the area where the musicians sit and is located between the "apron" (or part of the stage which juts out beyond the proscenium curtain— where dancers stand to take their final bows) and the first row of the audience. The "pit" derives its name from being on a lower level, to avoid obstructing the audience's view of the dancing.

The **conductor**, who not only leads the orchestra but also takes cues from the dancers, will bow and then begin either the overture (if it is a full-length ballet) or the music for the first dance. After the second intermission, the conductor will motion the orchestra to rise and take a bow. This is their time to be acknowledged, since they are hidden in the pit all evening.

Other standard moments to applaud include: after a series of *fouetté* turns by the ballerina, after a series of leaps across the stage or in a circle by the danseur, after an extraordinary balance by the ballerina or an extremely complicated lift by a couple in a *pas de deux* (a dance for two).

Certainly it is legitimate to applaud if a particular dancer is pleasing. Usually the audience applauds at the end of a solo. Sometimes this is within the body of a dance that continues as the soloist exits without acknowledging the audience. In classical ballet, it is traditional for the action of the dance to stop while the soloist comes back onstage to take a bow. Occasionally, in a full-length ballet such as *Swan Lake*, the principals may return center stage several times for bows before the orchestra continues the music. This can be annoying to those more accustomed to symphony procedure because it cuts into the dramatic continuity. But it is a tradition, and you're not obligated to applaud if it bothers you.

There are other less cut-and-dried moments when applause is certainly welcome, as when a dancer does a particularly difficult maneuver exceptionally well, or performs an unusual step with particular brilliance. In these cases, the audience is allowed to applaud whenever it likes. The portion on Dance Steps from the chapter "Dancers," gives information about what is good and what is difficult and should therefore serve as a guide to deciding when to applaud. Keep in mind, however, that it is always your decision when to applaud—it doesn't matter what those seated around you are doing. If you think the dancer is deserving, then applaud. It is also permissible to shout "bravo" during the curtain calls.

There is another dance tradition for praising the performers: the presentation of flowers onstage after a performance. During the final curtain call of the evening, ushers may come onstage and present certain dancers with flowers. A "curtain call" is what occurs each time the curtain goes up after the dance is finished. Usually curtain calls are choreographed, that is, the dancers take their bows in a preordained order and fashion. In a large classical ballet company, there will be a curtain call just for the *corps de ballet*. Then, the corps will stand at the back, while each soloist takes a bow, usually in order of importance. Lastly, the principals enter, take their individual bows, and then motion the entire company to walk forward for a final bow. At this point, the conductor will join the dancers onstage. If there is an instrumental soloist for a certain piece of dance music, this musician will also come up onstage and take a bow with the dancers.

In a modern dance company, generally each dancer will take an individual bow, either in a personal style or one choreographed by the director. Sometimes, these bows are in order of importance in the dance, with those who danced solos or lead roles last; or, if there is no hierarchical separation, each dancer will take a separate bow, or bow with partners.

Similar to opera, it is also traditional for the audience to throw small bouquets of flowers from the house. If you wish to do this, you have to run from your seat down the aisle and stand next to the orchestra pit and then aim well so that the flowers get over the orchestra to the feet of the dancers. This gesture is a courtesy to a dancer you particularly admire. The large bouquets presented by hand onstage are left at the stage door before the performance begins with a note attached. You can ask any usher in the theater where the stage door is. This entrance to the backstage usually has a security guard who will take your message or your flowers, but will not allow you to enter.

However, audience members may stand outside the stage door after the performance to see dancers leave the theater. Be prepared to wait for a while, however, as dancers usually shower and remove makeup before leaving. If you wish to ask for an autograph, have your program and a pen ready. Be courteous about the dancer's time, and remember that every performer—even the most celebrated—appreciates a compliment, especially if you can be specific. If you are refused an autograph, don't be dismayed. The dancers may be very tired and hungry, as many do not eat before a performance. And, consider that they have to get up early the next morning for class and to prepare for another performance. It is surprising how different dancers look offstage, so you may have difficulty recognizing your favorites as they leave the theater in street clothes.

Viewer etiquette also includes not talking during the ballet. Remember to shut off any alarms on your watch so as not to disturb the people seated around you. And, please, please, don't open candy or lozenge wrappers during the performance. This is terribly distracting to others in the audience. Your program will tell you not to use recording devices or flash cameras as well. Most theaters require cameras to be checked. A flashbulb could momentarily blind dancers, and perhaps result in injury.

If you are late to the theater, you will not be seated until an intermission or program pause. Walking down an aisle after the lights are dimmed is a distraction to the performers as well as rude to the other members of the audience. You will have to stand at the back and be seated by an usher during intermission. Sometimes the back of each section of the theater is reserved for "standees." These are people who have bought standing-room tickets. They may line up as many as ten deep to watch a favorite ballet from the back. This area is not such a bad spot for watching—since you're standing, there are no heads to block your view. And, the back of the theater is generally the most "raked" (the gradual uphill slant from row to row beginning at the orchestra), so that you're elevated slightly above the stage and can see the dancers' feet quite well.

The **house** is divided into various **sections** where the ticket prices vary: ORCHESTRA, or main floor; BOX SEATS—the first level up; and BALCONY. The terms referring to intermediate sections vary from theater to theater but usually include some of the following: loge, dress circle, mezzanine, balcony circle, first and second balcony.

The **stage** itself is divided into proscenium, apron, and wings. The PROSCENIUM ARCH is the area that separates the stage from the house. The APRON is the segment of the stage floor that juts out toward the audience; it is separated from the dancing portion of the stage by the proscenium curtain and is generally used in dance performances only when the performers take their curtain calls. The PROSCENIUM CURTAIN is the one that rises to begin the dance and lowers to end it. Behind and on either side of the proscenium are the WINGS. These several sections are separated by heavy black velvet curtains. Occasionally scenery divides the wings. The importance of wings for dancing is that they serve for entrances and exits: one group of dancers can exit offstage at the wing closest to the audience while another group is simultaneously entering from a wing at the back. The curtain across the back which sets off the performance area from the backstage area is either a blank BACKDROP or a large curtain upon which scenery is painted.

Finally, it is useful to know **stage directions** when referring to where dancing took place. These are designated as if you were the performer looking out at the audience, so you have to think in terms of opposite directions when you are seated in the audience. In other words, STAGE RIGHT is the performer's right as the dancer faces the audience, so it would be the audience's left. STAGE LEFT is the audience's right. CENTER STAGE should be obvious, and finally, UP and DOWN come from the time when all stages were RAKED, which means they were slanted from top to bottom toward the audience. Actors had to walk *down*hill to go toward the audience and *up*hill when walking away from the audience. Later, raking was eliminated in favor of a flat stage surface, which is much easier to dance upon. (In the Soviet Union and parts of Europe, companies still perform on raked stages.) This old tradition has remained in the expressions UP-STAGE and DOWNSTAGE, which refer to going away from and toward the audience respectively. If a dancer finishes a series of leaps at the edge of the stage closest to you and on your left, he has performed these leaps in a DOWNSTAGE RIGHT direction.

The **program** contains items of useful information for watching the performance.

You don't have to read the program carefully in order to understand the dance. Sometimes a performance is enjoyed even more without preparation of any kind, letting the mind be open and receptive to whatever happens onstage. For this type of experience, try not reading the program at all.

The first line of the title page of the program usually tells who is presenting the dance company. A PRESENTER is an individual or organization who backs the performances financially and provides the advertising, theater, support services, and personnel necessary to a production. After the name of the presenter (there may be more than one) is the name of the dance company, followed by its artistic director, primary choreographer, and other major administrators.

The titles of these personnel differ from company to company, but in general, the ARTISTIC DIRECTOR is the head decision-maker in the company and may also, but not necessarily, be the primary choreographer of works for the company. For instance, in the Joffrey Ballet, Gerald Arpino is the artistic director. This position—slightly different in function from company to company—has to do with daily administration of the company: the setting up of the performance season, choosing casts, deciding upon repertory. At New York City Ballet, Peter Martins is called Ballet Master-in-Chief (although his function is similar to that of artistic director). Martins is assisted by ballet masters. The BALLET MASTER (who can also be a woman, or BALLET MISTRESS) is responsible for supervising rehearsals, checking that new casts are dancing correctly, that the choreography is being performed accurately, and teaching dances to new casts. (In a company with more than one ballet master or mistress, each is assigned a certain number of ballets in the repertoire.)

The ballet master may be assisted by a REGISSEUR. This position covers all the day-to-day, nitty-gritty administrative work, such as posting the rehearsal schedule and casting according to the artistic director's dictates; coordinating rehearsal studios; and handling last-minute problems such as locating substitutes for injured dancers. Not all companies have regisseurs, but these duties must be handled by someone on the staff—perhaps the ballet master, rehearsal assistant, or choreographer's assistant. In a small modern dance company, it may be that the choreographer is also artistic director and rehearsal director. This is all information made clear on the title page of the program.

Some other important personnel are also listed here. It's worth taking a brief look; though the dancers may get most of your attention, these are the people that get them on that stage. The conductor(s) are named, as well as the musical director if these positions are separate. When they are, the musical director's duties differ from those of the conductor in that they include overseeing all the coordination between stage and pit. The choreographer may make cuts in the music, or a dancer may request a tempo change, both of which must be communicated to the orchestra. The musical director, or chief conductor, would also determine the accompanist needed for class and rehearsals, and work with instrumental soloists for specific pieces.

Finally, the title page of the program includes those involved in artistic design: sets, costumes, and lighting. These items are essential to the whole dance-going picture, though they are often so integrally woven into the final performance that it is easy to forget, or at least downplay, their importance. Many times a different designer is chosen for each dance; in some companies there is a resident lighting designer who LIGHTS (or creates the lighting for) every dance.

Within the program itself will be listed each dance, the dancers performing in it, and everything else needed to mount it onstage: the specific choreographer; lighting, costume, and set designer(s); the conductor, composer, and perhaps the arranger, or orchestrator, if the original score has been modified for the dance. It will also include any information the choreographer wishes to share, perhaps a paragraph of explanation, or a quote that inspired the piece. In a dance that tells a story, the plot will be summarized. If the dance is broken down into sections, dancers for each will be listed, usually with the soloists, or those dancing lead parts, named first with a slight separation between their names and the others. This may not be important unless you have come to see a certain dancer or if you wish to learn the names of dancers you like. One way to handle the latter is to mark your program at intermission, after seeing the performance. Then, in future performances of the same company, you may choose to come on the night that a particular dancer is going to perform.

A few other more unusual items may also appear in the program notes, including comments such as "courtesy of" or "staged by." These refer to where or from what company the dance originated, and are more likely to be seen in a large ballet company program. For instance, the ballet may be borrowed from the company where it was originally produced and, if it includes the loan of scenery and/or costumes, then it would say, COURTESY OF. . . . In the case of, say, a Balanchine ballet, it may have been taught to the company by a former Balanchine dancer, in which case the program will state STAGED BY. . . .

There may also be a brief statement thanking a certain individual for a donation that made the production possible, as well as indicating the grants and gifts that were used to finance the production. Another item of interest is the details of the first performance of the work. If the piece were premiered in an earlier performance, the date and place of that performance, as well as the principal dancers, will be indicated, primarily for historical interest.

Dance performances are usually divided into three parts, which allow both dancers and audience breaks throughout the evening. In modern dance companies, there will usually be three dances presented, with an intermission or a pause between each. In most ballet performances, there will either be a full-length ballet, with intermissions between each act, or an evening of repertory consisting of three or four diverse works, presented with an intermission between each.

REPERTORY refers to all the dances that a company can perform. Works from that repertory are presented at different times during the performing season or at different cities on tour. Repertory can shift year by year, with some works being withdrawn from the current repertory while premieres are added. Later, former dances may be revived, restaged, or remounted. REVIVED simply refers to bringing the piece back into the active repertory, similar to bringing a painting out for exhibition from the permanent collection.

If RESTAGED, the work is either being brought from another company where it was originally created, or it has been reworked by the company choreographer in a slightly different form. A new production of an old work, such as **Baryshnikov's** *Swan Lake* for American Ballet Theatre (ABT) is referred to as being "restaged," since Baryshnikov added his own choreography and changed other aspects of this classical ballet.

Restaged is not too different from REMOUNTING, which usually refers to a change by the choreographer when setting the production on a new group of dancers or a new company. A work is also considered remounted when the costumes and set are upgraded. Sometimes a company presents an old work from repertory with the same choreography but adds new costumes or scenery.

Quite often the middle section of an evening's program consists of two shorter pieces or *divertissements* (solos and *pas de deux*). These dances will be separated by a pause, which differs from an intermission in that the lights come up dimly so that you can see to read your program, but not long enough to leave your seat. These pauses are usually to prepare the stage or change the backdrop between dances. The term *divertissements* also refers to segments taken from longer dances that are presented on their own, such as the *Don Quixote pas de deux* (featured near the end of the film *The Turning Point*), taken from the full-length ballet also called *Don Quixote*.

Sometimes the dancers take bows after each act of a full-length ballet, much like the opera, and sometimes they wait until the end of the evening. In a program consisting of three pieces separated by intermissions, there will be choreographed curtain calls after each dance before the intermission since the same dancers may not appear again later in the evening or those in leading roles may shift.

If there is to be any change in the order of the program or who is dancing what, this change will be announced before the houselights dim. It is handy to have a pencil ready to mark the changes in your program at this time. There's no need to be unduly disappointed if a dance or dancer you were anticipating doesn't appear. This could be an opportunity to discover someone new whose talent hadn't been noticed before. The person listed in the "first cast" for a dance is not always the one you'll love most. Sometimes there is an up-and-comer whose personality will whisk you away. The assumption that the best dancers appear on opening night for the critics' reviews, and newcomers are broken in at matinees, isn't necessarily true. And, after all, you may find that your favorite dancers are not those of the artistic director. Or, you may enjoy the prospect of discovering some new talent, perhaps hidden in the *corps de ballet*. Many a shining career has begun with a quick substitution for an injured principal.

The unrecognized have the same training and rehearsal—they just haven't had their break yet. You may get to witness it. And, remember, dancers' bows aren't popularity contests. An audience favorite may not be given leading roles by dance company administration. You may also disagree with a critic's choice. Trust your own judgment. Those in the background today may be center stage tomorrow.

HISTORY AND TRADITIONS

At one time, everybody danced. Holidays and all special occasions were celebrated by dancing. Children learned the dances that were passed along from generation to generation. Folk dancing, therefore, is the origin of all theater dance, whether ballet or modern, Broadway show dancing or jazz and tap.

Dancing per se, however, had its origins even further back than village or folk dances. Man danced before he could talk. Body language—the root of dancing—was the communication of the cave man. The hunt was enacted before warriors left the tribe and the desired outcome was danced for the good harvest of crops. Finally, early man celebrated his victories in the hunt, the harvest, and in protecting himself against the forces of nature and other tribes, with ritual dances. American Indian dances are an example of this time in the history of dance when movement was used for a specific, more utilitarian purpose. Symbolism was important, and masks, costumes, and props were eventually incorporated to elaborate upon the steps.

Folk dances took on more complex forms when revised for the aristocracy. These court dances were also originally designed to be danced by everyone. An important part of every child's education was dance instruction. All parties included social dances, which tended to differ from folk dances of the villagers only in their formality. In part, this look was the result of the ornate dress of the day, but it also had to do with court protocol and etiquette.

Not meant to be a professional performance, dance was exhibited by the nobility for and with their peers. Social dances such as the minuet began to be set in patterns around the room so as to be more interesting to watch. No more skill was required to perform these early dances than most courtiers had been taught in order to participate in formal balls and parties.

At the time when dancing began to shift from being something everyone *did* to something aristocrats *watched*, elaborate garb was in vogue. Towering headdresses and heeled shoes for both sexes, heavy skirts held out by hoops with layers of underskirts for the women, embellished waistcoats with trousers buttoned at the knee for men—these stiff garments resulted in fairly stiff movements. The attire, in other words, made the choreography. The performers were far too hampered by their clothing to get off the ground very much and too encumbered to perform intricate—or quick—steps.

The transition to dance as a performance instead of mere entertainment for the royalty occurred primarily at the behest of Louis XIV. The Sun King loved to dance and held gigantic *masques* as often as possible at his elegant Versailles. However, he also loved to eat—and soon his girth made his own dancing impossible. He therefore decided that if he were going to have to sit by and watch dancing, others should too. He set about creating dancing entertainments that he and other members of his court could observe. For this purpose, he designed a large ballroom floor with a balcony that ran around all four

LOUIS XIV IN PERFORMANCE

sides. Thus the first dances were looked "down" upon (nearly the opposite of today's audiences). Because of this seating arrangement, the steps and patterns of the dances began to change as well. Dances needed to be interesting to watch, not just fun to perform.

In fact, this difference in the enjoyment of doing versus watching is often an important quality to notice in current choreography. If you are bored while watching, but the performers appear to be enjoying themselves, then the choreography may be at fault. Some movement feels fun to do, but doesn't look that interesting on the stage.

As time went by, Louis XIV became more ambitious about dance as theater entertainment and founded the Academie Royale de Danse in 1661 to objectify standards and codify court and character dances. Although this group was defunct by 1780, the Academie Royale de Musique, 1671, which later became the Paris Opera, had an associated school for training dance professionals that has continued uninterrupted to the present day. Because the Sun King's school was the first to write down the names of the steps, ballet vocabulary dates from this time. The universal language of dance is still French.

For the purposes of viewing, however, specific details of who did what and when and with whom or with what dance step are not essential. The critical importance of dance history is how the aspects of the times shaped the dancing. Ballet has been off-putting to many because of its aristocratic, seemingly artificial aspects. Ballet can appear to be haughty, incomprehensible, or, perhaps most often, inaccessible. But understanding its origins and the development of its traditions might help the viewer make better sense of ballet's rather formal aspects.

If you keep in mind the fact that all primitive tribes communicated to one another through dance, performances become less mystical. Theater dance is simply a clarification and projection of what is organic about movement so that it can be appreciated and understood by the viewing audience. Choreographers and dancers, rather than obscuring with various styles, are, in fact, working to mold years and years of the evolution of dance into a form that is accessible to all hearts that beat. Human beings experience emotions that they wish to share with one another. Dancing on a stage is one way to do that. And it ought to do that even if someone sitting in the audience doesn't know the history or the technique.

Many of the prescriptions of ballet date back to traditions begun in Louis XIV's court (and some back even further, to the courts of the late sixteenth century). For instance, since

the audience sat above the ballroom, *patterns* about the floor
were more important than intricate *steps*; and the interaction
between partners was emphasized to increase the interest of
movements. Because theater dance developed out of social
dances which anyone could do, and because royalty—not
professionals—were the performers, early steps were kept
simple.

Most important, it should be remembered that the development of dance steps was profoundly affected by clothing.
Costumes for dance performances originally copied the court
fashion then in vogue. Apparel also created the difference
between men's and women's steps. While women in the
French court wore floor-length skirts, men were attired in
doublet, waistcoast, and breeches, with hose covering the calf
of the leg. Since their legs were not only visible but also more
free than women's, men developed more technically dazzling
feats.

As jumping was considered an impropriety, the only time
women got off the ground was when they were lifted by men.
Even this was rare, because the weight of all her garments
made a lady quite a load. Additionally, a particularly high lift
could prove embarrassing—until "precautionary drawers"
were invented. Women were further encumbered by corsets,
which may be the origin of ballet's characteristically stiff,
upright torso. Shoulder bands on corsets at the turn of the
seventeenth century restrained the arms so that choreography
was restricted to the forearms, hands, and fingers.

While men might sport a pair of trousers fastened with
garters at the knee, women's skirts were fanned out by FAR-
THINGALES, or hoop skirts, and PANNIERS, a light framework
for extending a dress from the hips. By the 1720s, men too
had adapted the hoop in the form of a TONNELET, or scalloped
skirt that reached just above the knee and extended nearly
the width of a man's extended arms.

Dressed in contemporary fashion instead of costume appropriate to the origin of the piece being performed, a dancer would indicate period, style, or character by an identifying prop (such as a lyre to suggest Greece, a fan for Spain). These props were another factor determining the type of dance choreography in early ballets—the only movements staged were those that could be executed with a prop in hand.

In the beginning of professional dance, like the theater, all roles were taken by males. The first professional ballerina is thought to be **Mademoiselle Lafontaine**, who made her debut in 1681, although she was prevented from any sort of virtuosity by the requisite heavy, floor-length skirt. It's little wonder that men at first surpassed women technically. Their snug-fitting silk hose allowed freedom of articulation for the legs, while women's legs were hidden in layers of skirts. Men at this time began experimenting with *pirouettes*, or turns, and *batterie*, or quick foot moves off the ground.

This segregation of the sexes changed drastically with the Paris Opéra debut (1726) of **Marie-Anne de Aupis de Camargo**. When a male dancer failed to appear for his solo in a 1730 performance, Camargo swiftly danced it in his stead. In spite of her skirt, she proved that women were equally capable of *allegro* (fast) footwork.

Camargo's *tour de force* heralded the ascendency of the female, which culminated in the nineteenth century. She is credited with shortening her skirt to an inch or two above the ankle so that the audience could more easily see her *entrechat quatre*, from French for "four," or *quatre*, "beats," or exchanges of the feet around the ankles.

Legend has it that Camargo also removed the heels from her shoes so that she could get a better spring into the air. By thus enabling the entire foot to make firm contact with the ground in a preparatory *plié* or knee bend, Camargo and the dancers succeeding her began mastering the air. ÉLÉVA-

TION, as aerial technique is called, however, has yet remained a specialty of the male dancer up to today. Perhaps this is due to the head start he got in the eighteenth century when women were still earthbound in their cumbersome dresses.

The changing role of women called for more adjustments of the basic costume. As her skirt billowed with air during a leap, the professional female dancer was likely to reveal more of her leg than she intended. Hence precautionary drawers. It's a shame they weren't invented before one of Camargo's colleagues caught her skirt on the scenery and was applauded more for her anatomical display than her technical prowess.

Another contemporary of Camargo, **Marie Sallé**, concerned with matching her costume to the character she was portraying, was the first to do away with both corset and headdress. Sallé wore flowing Greek-style robes and let her hair fall loosely about her shoulders, similar to the fashion popularized by Isadora Duncan.

With this change, skirts became gradually softer. They remained "Camargo" length, but the panniers that extended the skirt were left behind as the 1700s drew to a close. Once again, stage costuming was reflecting social dress—gauzy draperies were the height of feminine fashion in the 1800s. The fabric of women's wear in both dance costumes and general dress matched the ushering in of the ideals and temperament of the Romantic era.

In the ballet world, the 1830s through the 1850s saw the flowering of the ballerina. The ethereal and the exotic were the subject matter for ballets about unattainable women who were often sprites or spirits that flew about the air, sought after by yearning, if insipid, young men. Enhanced by technical innovations in theater design, which permitted lowering the houselights during the performance, drawing the curtain between scenes, and varying the intensity of onstage illumination with the advent of gas lighting, staged performance took on a dreamy quality replete with mist and supernatural spirits.

The ballet that may have started the movement toward the supremacy of the ballerina was *La Sylphide*, premiered in 1832. The leading lady, **Marie Taglioni**, created such a sensation that Parisian women copied her hair and made *Taglioniser* a verb. Taglioni wore a diaphanous multilayered white skirt that reached just below the knee, and her hair was pulled back into a bun. Both hairstyle and skirt became associated with what are still known today as "romantic" ballets.

The TUTU developed from the costume of Taglioni and became standard as the Romantic era blossomed. It was a buoyant skirt constructed of layers of tarlatan, silk or nylon, which undulated gracefully as the ballerina danced, adding to the impression that she was a creature of the air. Today a ROMANTIC-LENGTH TUTU refers to a skirt reaching anywhere from knee length to just above the ankle. Attached is a simple white bodice, secured over the shoulders with straps of elastic. Thus is the entire arm and shoulder area bared for greater freedom and ease of movement.

Hair, for this romantic style, is parted in the middle, drawn down over the ears and secured in a bun at the nape of the neck. Sometimes a wreath of tiny flowers encircles the head. Puff sleeves of net, secured by elastic, sometimes are worn midway along the upper arm.

Many of the ballets choreographed during this Romantic period (such as *Giselle*, 1841) are known today as WHITE BAL-LETS, so named after the long white tutus worn by the bal-lerinas. *Ballets blancs* would also include the plotless ballet *Les Sylphides*, seen in the repertory of American Ballet Theatre, which was originally choreographed by Michel Fokine in Rus-sia in 1907 as an homage to the Romantic era.

Costuming for the danseur also became standardized in the Romantic ballets. He wore white tights—a natural evolution

THE ROMANTIC TUTU

from the courtier's silk hose—which covered the legs from toes to waist. On his upper torso was a full-sleeved, billowy blouse with either vest, jacket, or a soft bow tying at the neck. For most classical ballets even today, men wear some variation of this costume from the Romantic era.

Shoes meanwhile softened from heeled street shoes into slippers of glovelike leather that conformed to the shape of the foot. This suppleness allowed the full extension of the foot into a point, executed by stretching the metatarsal arch—the one in the ball of the foot—as well as the arch in the center of the foot. (The opposing position to this is the flexed foot, such as that achieved while standing flat-footed on the ground.) The shoe's flexibility permitted increased intricacy of steps, allowing both dancers and choreographers to experiment with greater complexity of movement. Soft leather made the landing of the body almost noiseless, thus enhancing the supernatural quality of Romantic era ballets.

TECHNIQUE SLIPPERS

Known today as the ballet slipper, or TECHNIQUE SLIPPER, the advantage to this shoe is that it fits like a second skin. The next best thing to being barefoot, the ballet slipper also protects the foot from the floor and provides a smooth surface on which to spin. (The bare foot tends to stick to the floor and slow down the motion.) This shoe also gives the dancer maximum contact with the floor for a secure base before taking off into the air. Thus were male dancers able to enlarge their repertory of aerial maneuvers.

No one knows exactly when or how the phenomenon began that was to revolutionize ballet, but one day in the early 1800s, a female dancer lifted herself to the very tips of her toes— quite a precarious balance considering how soft her slippers were. Being *sur les pointes*, however, was so effective for the chimerical roles of the ballerina in the Romantic era that women were soon devising ways of staying up there longer and doing more while there.

"Toe" dancing developed as a theatrically appropriate movement style. Although *pointe* shoes would later metamorphose dramatically the female dancer's technique, their most important immediate effect was to establish the delicate characterizations of the fanciful plots of romantic ballets. From apparitions to sylphs, *pointe* work suggested the floating of airy spirits. The idealized female was all the more inaccessible because she defied the laws of gravity. Steps on *pointe* presented the illusion of floating across the stage.

This impression was magnified by the gossamer white tutu and may explain why the ballerina is conventionally garbed in pale pink or white. The traditional pink tights and pink satin *pointe* shoes match the pale arms of the typical Romantic ballerina, who could hardly have a ruddy complexion when portraying an airborne sprite in *La Sylphide*, or the spirit of a dead girl in the ballet *Giselle*. With the advent of stage lighting, white tutu, pink tights, and pale skin combined to make the ballerina all the more ethereal.

The arrival of the *pointe* shoe also turned the tables on the theatrical battle of the sexes, as the ballerina's toes eclipsed the male's virtuoso leaping. He became a mere *porteur* for the graceful lady, lifting her into flight, supporting her balance on those precarious *pointes*, and carrying her delicate body about the stage. Ballet scenarios continued this theme, with the development of dance technique focusing on the woman in her newly created shoes.

As the 1800s progressed, female dancers constantly improved the design of their soft *pointe* shoes. Technical innovations required that the feet have more support, so the toes of the *pointe* shoe were darned with stiff threads in a crisscross pattern and the sides and ends of the slipper were reinforced with stitched ribbons. During the 1860s, *blocked* shoes were developed—the area surrounding the toes was stiffened with layers of glue or starch.

By the mid-nineteenth century, when the Romantic era had run its course, the male was left with almost nothing to do onstage. Men's roles were even danced by women—a far cry from the mid-seventeenth century when the reverse was true. A ballet created in 1870, and still performed by major companies, *Coppélia*, was originally danced with the hero *en travesti*. **Gerald Arpino**, Artistic Director of the Joffrey Ballet, suggests that women's *pointe* shoes castrated the male in ballet. For nearly a century, the male figure was relegated to ridiculous roles from impotent noblemen yearning after diaphanously clad females in the first half of the nineteenth century, to mice, cabbages, and butterflies in the tawdry spectacle ballets of the late nineteenth century. (An exception was the Royal Danish Ballet, where Bournonville choreography, which emphasized the male "ballon," or bounce, flourished in isolation.)

But as the Romantic movement was dying out in the West, the Imperial Ballet of Russia was setting a rigid standard from which it never deviated. The increasingly complex technique for *pointe* shoes found fertile ground in Russia in the second half of the nineteenth century. Advances in dance technique caused more costuming changes. Legs in the Russian school were raised ever higher with increased technical advancement, until a *développé* (or opening of the leg from a bent to a straight position away from the body), which at one time was considered correct at waist level, was now up as high as the dancer's arms or shoulders. To accommodate these changes, the tutu was shortened until it stood out almost perpendicular at the waist, thus baring the entire leg.

This tutu was also a one-piece outfit, with little panties and a simple bodice attached to the stiff skirt. Hairstyles also made the transition to a more aristocratic look, with the bun placed higher on the head, hair pulled severely back straight from the face, and a coronet or tiara crowning all.

Dating from the latter half of the nineteenth century, this look is called CLASSICAL as opposed to the style conveyed by the longer romantic-length tutu. The shorter tutu stayed conveniently out of the way during lifts, and allowed for more elaborate partnering, such as shoulder sits and fish dives.

Another development of the emerging "classical" ballet in Imperial Russia, was the four-act dramatic ballet. Based on fairy tales, myths or legends, ballets such as *Don Quixote* (1869), *The Sleeping Beauty* (1890), and *Nutcracker* (1892) were elaborate productions. Huge casts of characters gave ample opportunity for every dancer to display individual prowess in technically demanding solos. The art of *pas de deux*, or partner dancing, soared to new heights also as a result of this story format, resulting in the standard "formula" used today —entrée and adagio, solo variation for each dancer, coda and finale.

But the displays of virtuosity permitted by *pointe* work and shortened tutus had little to do with the plot, or the dramatic "scenario" of the choreography. This infuriated **Michel Fokine**, who rebelled against the Imperial Russian Ballet when he joined Diaghilev's Ballets Russes in 1909 as a choreographer. "Pointes," according to the perceptive Fokine, "should be used as a means and not the sole aim of ballet. Pointes should be employed where they are suitable and renounced

THE CLASSICAL TUTU

without regret where they should not serve any artistic purpose. For instance, in Eastern ballets, the bare foot or a soft shoe is more pleasing than a ballet shoe, but the dancer in *Le Cygne* [The Swan], does not offend when she uses her pointes to suggest a soaring movement. It is right if all her body express the same feeling, but wrong if she uses her pointes to display her 'steel' toes . . . a horrible invention of the ballet in decline. In its days of greatness, supernatural lightness was the ideal. Now, the steel toes, hard legs and precision in execution, are the ideals."

The heyday of the Imperial Russian Ballet (middle to end of the nineteenth century), culminated virtuoso technique and lavish productions. Many of the large-scale ballets performed today were first mounted, choreographed, and designed during this period, while the rigid training programs that produced so many world-class stars began to be established. Whereas French ballet had been supreme since the time of Louis XIV (Paris Opera ballet masters were imported to Russia and Italy), and Italian ballerinas dominated Russian ballet productions in the late nineteenth century, Petipa's choreography established the prominence of Russian ballet that continued with the emigration of its greatest dancers to Diaghilev's Ballets Russes and later all over Europe.

However, such tremendous fertility also presaged the decline, in the early twentieth century, of ballet into burlesque and diversion. Anna Pavlova, for instance, danced in America as part of a pageant that included circus animals and aerial displays.

Most Americans at the turn of the century associated the word "dance" with music halls, tossing skirts, and high kicks. (Ballet's continued difficulty at establishing itself in America was also due to leftover puritan attitudes that considered dancing immoral, and the suspicion of a democratic society toward an art form created by the aristocracy.)

Meanwhile, would-be impresario, dilettante, and genius **Serge Diaghilev** began importing stars of the Russian ballet for Paris seasons involving outrageously innovative collaborations between major artists of the day, up-and-coming composers, and untried choreographic talent. The Ballets Russes (1909–1929), as his later company became known, boasted a roster of dancers including **Nijinsky**, **Pavlova**, **Karsavina**, **Fokine**, **Massine**, **Bolm**, **Lifar**, **Dolin**, **Balanchine**, **Danilova**, **Markova**. (Indeed, nearly all the big names in ballet history are listed as members of either Diaghilev's company or one of its successors.)

Costuming for the Diaghilev productions introduced audiences to Cubism (Picasso's *Parade*), the dazzling color of the exotic (*Schéhérazade*, *Firebird*), and the mixture of art with theatrical decor (Roerich's drops for *Le Sacre du Printemps*). Such artistic collaborations have been unmatched—before or since—in both magnitude and caliber.

After the dissolution of the company upon Diaghilev's death in 1929, the Diaghilev dancers reappeared in various companies whose names were perplexingly similar: **Ballet Russe de Monte Carlo**, Colonel de Basil's **Ballet Russe**, Rene Blum's **Ballets de Monte Carlo**, **Original Ballet Russe**, **Ballets Russes de Monte Carlo**. However, all these companies—along with Pavlova's tours (1910–1925)—were seminal in spreading ballet to America, continuing the careers of great figures in the history of dance, and allowing new choreography to flourish at a time when ballet throughout Europe had become stale.

(It is interesting to note that as most of the ballet talent had left Russia, and none as yet had been established in America, modern dance made its appearance.)

While at first company names were derivatives of "ballets russes," and most non-Russian dancers changed their names in acquiescence to the widespread belief that the only good ballet came from Russia, these emigré dancers later began settling in America and opening studios.

Out of this dispersion came America's **Mordkin Ballet**, whose members formed **Ballet Theatre**, which became **American Ballet Theatre** in 1940—a showcase of the classics well mixed with new "American" choreography, such as that of **de Mille**, **Robbins**, and **Loring**. ABT dancers included those from various assortments of balles russes, and later hosted some of the greatest names in ballet history: **Anton Dolin, Alicia Alonso, Alicia Markova, Nora Kaye, Hugh Laing, Sallie Wilson, Ivan Nagy, Natalia Makarova, Mikhail Baryshnikov, Gelsey Kirkland, Cynthia Gregory**.

By the time America produced its own ballet companies, costuming had again undergone a radical change commensurate with innovations in both dance technique and choreography. Former Diaghilev choreographer **George Balanchine** came to America in 1933 and later effected radical changes in performance dress that had everything to do with choreographic purpose. Balanchine created a sparse, technically demanding style of dance which has been dubbed "neo-classic."

His ballets had no plot, no characterizations, and often no decor. Balanchine's stage designs with moving bodies were intrinsically enmeshed with the music. His dancers wore the simplest possible clothing on an empty stage so that nothing detracted from the visual impact of the dancing body.

Balanchine's "rehearsal-clothes" ballets such as *Concerto Barocco* (1940) and *Agon* (1957), put ballerinas in pink tights and toe shoes, but gone were the elaborate tutus. His ladies wore tunics instead, as if they had just stepped away from the studio *barre* and onto the stage. Men also wore a practice uniform consisting of black tights contrasted with white ballet slippers, socks, and tee-shirts. The result was stark and dramatically effective. Audiences made little note of the clothing but they couldn't take their eyes off the dancers. Although he also choreographed elaborate productions with stunning costumes, Balanchine's modus operandi changed the focus of ballet from spectacle to pure dance.

Dance history is continually being made by choreographers and dancers new on the scene. Each season another young wonder makes his or her debut—and often this dancing may not be seen in another country. New dance companies spring up constantly. The difficult part about pinning all this down, however, is that small dance companies come and go, and some choreographers may shine only briefly. Meanwhile, new dancers develop greater technique, fresh choreographers create new styles, and dance history, while based on tradition, is continuously being changed.

MODERN DANCE

Originally, "modern dance" referred to the style of danc-ing that developed specifically as a revolt against ballet. As with any historical movement, modern dance evolved over a period of time. However, **Isadora Duncan**, who was active from 1899 to 1927, is often considered to have begun "modern dance."

The innovations of Isadora were preceded by some rebellion within the ballet world itself. As early as 1907, **Michel Fokine** had written his invective against the use of the toe shoe merely for technical display without regard for the dramatic action of the ballet. His ballets, such as *The Dying Swan*, *Les Sylphides*, and *Firebird*, evidence his concern that steps fit the dramatic purpose of the ballet. But whereas Fokine rebelled within the confines of the ballet idiom—modifying ballet for a more contemporary look—Isadora began by throwing out the old and starting a fresh style.

In historical context, it must be remembered that many of the elements that are considered hallmarks of modern dance had already been used in ballet choreography, such as bare feet, dancers reclining or kneeling on the floor, loose costum-ing instead of the standard tutu, and the commission of con-temporary composers.

This overlap of elements can be confusing when trying to separate the specifics that comprise modern dance. While there were some contemporary components to ballet choreography, the creators of modern dance wished to break free from the fixed confines of what is generally accepted as classical ballet.

At the time Isadora appeared on the dance scene, ballet in Europe had degenerated into fancy tricks and acrobatics. Choreography had been reduced to audience pleasers; dancers went for applause. The number of *pirouettes* performed had become more important than the way in which they were danced. As technique advanced, the soul had gone out of dancing.

Fokine attempted to make amends with more contemporary ballet choreography, but Isadora's desires took her one step further. She discarded in toto the vocabulary of ballet and its traditions. Instead of dancing with a stiff, upright torso, Isadora believed that all movement originated in the solar plexus, flowing out from that source into the rest of the body.

Isadora was influenced by classic Greek dress, lifestyle, and art, even copying images for her dances from Hellenistic vases. She also studied Italian paintings endlessly at the Louvre, and read prodigiously such writers as Descartes, Darwin, Rousseau, and Nietzsche. But music was her major inspiration for creating movement. Except in the Diaghilev company and the Imperial Ballet (not yet seen outside Russia), music written specifically for the ballet had deteriorated into simple melodies that functioned merely as background for competitive technical shows. She wanted to dance from the feelings and reactions that music engendered in her, so she used composers—such as Beethoven, Schubert, Chopin, Wagner, Scriabin, and Gluck—up to then considered appropriate only in the concert hall, and later the Russian composers with whom she felt in sympathy after touring their country. She also removed the trappings of ballet that, indeed, made her feel trapped—tutu, tights, and toe slippers.

For Isadora, dancing was a free expression of the individual. Therefore, she wanted her feet and body unencumbered. She often danced barefoot, clothed in flowing gowns that revealed her naked body underneath. These robes also allowed greater freedom of movement, especially in the upper torso. Unlike the creators of ballet, Isadora felt no necessity to strive for the illusion of perfection. She believed the human body to be beautiful as it was.

ISADORA IN COSTUME

Finally, because Isadora felt that *any* movement was appropriate to dance, she eliminated the codified steps and traditional positions of classical ballet. Her choreography consisted more of pure, "natural" physicality, including running, skipping, hopping, undulating the arms and torso, and a free use of the head, shoulders, and neck which, until then, had to conform to the predetermined positions of ballet.

Isadora let her body tell her what dancing was. She began her career with solo dances that described an exuberance and expressed the feelings that compelled her to move. Her magic was electrifying—due partly to her own charisma—to audiences who had grown tired of the dull circus show ballet had become.

As is generally the case with any new art form, in order to survive it had to become distilled into a format that could be passed along. While Isadora did not create a movement vocabulary per se, her schools of dance, where large groups of children were encouraged to dance free-form on the lawn in white tunics with garlands in their hair, were a vital part of what she felt to be her mission. Those students she adopted as daughters, called the "Isadorables," were instrumental in teaching her choreography after her death.

Isadora's primary legacy was an attitude about dance and the human body. Her historical importance lies not so much in specific technique as in the philosophy she promulgated, which had a profound influence not just on future modern dancers, but the world of ballet as well. (The extremely open and expansive *épaulement* of the Russian ballet technique, for instance, was influenced by Isadora.) While what remains today are primarily reconstructions of Isadora's choreography, her principles allowed dancers following in her footsteps to express themselves more naturally. (These individual voices later became movement techniques and choreographic styles.)

Modern dance developed almost simultaneously in Germany and America in such a manner that it is often difficult to pin down who influenced whom. This cross-fertilization of ideas affected both modern *and* ballet dancing. Characteristic of the early modern choreographers is that each created a style of movement and/or a technique different from anything that had been seen before, and that their styles persisted long enough to influence other dancers who choreographed later —hence the term "pioneers."

The movement forms that began modern dance occasionally seemed to evolve one out of another. For instance, **Mary**

Wigman (1886–1973) began a school of movement in Germany in 1920; in addition to choreographing group pieces for her pupils, she was also a riveting soloist in dramatic works using masks and weighty movements, creating dances that she believed to be functional instead of diverting, and free from dependence on musical accompaniment.

One of her pupils, **Hanya Holm** (b. 1898), was sent to America to open a Wigman school in 1931. In the process, Holm created her own company and a distinctive technique —based, of course, on Wigman. Influenced by German expressionism in the arts, Holm technique included dramatic gestures, symbolic movement, and percussion as the accompaniment, especially in class. On the flip side, Holm was also capable of lighter movement; in addition to directing opera, she also choreographed *Kiss Me Kate*, *My Fair Lady*, and *Camelot*, insisting upon the complete integration of the dance into the dramatic action.

Concurrently, another student of Wigman, **Harald Kreutzberg** (1902–1968), was choreographing pieces combining free dance with drama in Germany. Although originally a member of a ballet company, Kreutzberg became known as the leading male exponent of modern dance in Germany, later touring America with his dancing partner, his shaven head a hallmark.

Simultaneously, a German ballet choreographer, **Kurt Jooss** (1901–1979), was attempting to synthesize classical and modern dance forms in strongly theatrical ballets with contemporary ideas. As an example, his most lasting piece is the antiwar *The Green Table* (1932), set on ballet—not modern dance—companies, but performed in ballet slippers, not *pointe* shoes.

While modern dancers had in common a desire to return to the freer, more natural movement that started theatrical dancing in the first place, there also appears to be a similarity in influence. **Hanya Holm** studied with Jaques-Dalcroze; her American contemporary, **Ruth St. Denis**, studied with Delsarte.

Emile Jaques-Dalcroze (1865–1950), was a Swiss music teacher and theoretician. His *gymnastique rhythmique* was a system of training musical sensibility through the translation of rhythm into bodily movements, or what became known as *eurythmics*. In addition to Holm, his influential pupils included Holm's teacher, **Mary Wigman**, who left him—as did Jooss —to study with Laban.

In addition to inventing a lasting system of dance notation, **Rudolf Laban** (1879–1958) worked out his theories with massive movement "choirs." *Choreutics*, the analysis of human movement in terms of twelve directions derived from the points of the icosahedron (the crystal form nearest to the sphere) and *eukinectics*, or controlling the dynamics and expression of the body, led to changes in both dramatic dance and the relation of the dancer to space.

François Delsarte (1811–1871) formulated a system for teaching control of body movements by analyzing the gestures of the human body as expressions of the emotional states. He divided movements into three categories—eccentric, concentric, and normal—and expressions into three zones—head, torso, and limbs; and human behavior into three attitudes— mental, moral, and vital. His theories, along with the teaching of his pupil **Jaques-Dalcroze**, strongly influenced the pioneers of modern dance, among them **Ted Shawn** (1891–1972) who, with his wife, Ruth St. Denis, established the first American school of modern dance in Los Angeles.

Created in 1915, Denishawn, as first school and then performing company, became synonymous with modern dance in America. Nearly all the originators of early modern dance companies either studied or performed with Denishawn, among them **Martha Graham, Doris Humphrey, Charles Weidman**.

Ruth St. Denis (1880–1968), having appeared previously in the New York music hall productions of David Belasco, performed her first ballet in 1906—her choreography, costumes, and style all inspired by an arresting cigarette poster of the Egyptian goddess Isis. She went on that year to perform her ballets *Radha, Dance of the Five Senses, The Incense,* and *The Cobras* so successfully her European tour lasted for three years. *The Nautch, Yogi,* and *Egypta* were created for her first United States tour in 1909, all based on her fascination with the Oriental, both in movement and philosophy.

As dancer, choreographer, teacher, and theorist, Miss Ruth (as she came to be known) attempted to make music visible through dance, rather like **Jaques-Dalcroze**. Drawing her inspiration mainly from Eastern art, her later dances increasingly reflected her religious and spiritual beliefs, such as the integration of body and soul. (She founded the Society of Spiritual Arts, whose aim was to synthesize religious motivation and artistic decoration.)

During the same years, on the opposite coast, **Ted Shawn** had started his own school. (He first performed in 1911, and appeared in one of the first known dance films, *Dance of the Ages*.) While touring with his own company in 1914, he met Miss Ruth. Their subsequent marriage was also to become a wedding of dance styles. "Denishawn" dancers toured— often in the vaudeville circuit—until 1932, when the couple separated.

Characterized by huge pageants, Oriental and ethnic dance influences, and a somewhat vague—occasionally inauthentic —blending of style, philosophy, and technique, the Denishawn legacy was primarily the training of an entire generation of modern dance choreographers who started their own companies after experience performing with the company and thereby being introduced to a smattering of nearly all dance forms, including Miss Ruth's fascination with India, Japan, and Spain, and Shawn's specialty in American folk dance, as well as investigations of German modern dance, manipulation of veils and scarves, experiments with music visualizations, and even ballet.

In 1933, Ted Shawn opened Jacob's Pillow, a center for performance and dance training in western Massachusetts, where his company—the All-Male Dancers Group—was in residence. Continuing long after his death in 1972, the Jacob's Pillow Dance Festival was, and is, distinguished by its open-mindedness to all forms of dance—classical, modern, jazz, and ethnic.

While his movement technique is not codified, Ted Shawn did have a specific philosophy of dance, which he expounded in his many books: *Gods Who Dance*, *Every Little Movement*, *The American Ballet*, *Fundamentals of a Dance Education*, *Dance We Must*, *One Thousand and One Night Stands*. Shawn continued to perform well into the 1960s and is recognized particularly as the first champion of the male dancer, creating athletic and virtuoso choreography to overcome the prejudices about the male dancer's perceived effeminancy. He used to say that every American should have to stand naked in Times Square one day a year—then America would be a nation of beautiful bodies.

Doris Humphrey (1895–1958), danced with the Denishawn company from 1917 to 1928. While she started choreographing for herself in 1920, she formed a performing group in 1928 with **Charles Weidman**. Her choreography was various and eclectic: Bach, *Air for the G String*, *Passacaglia in C Minor*; contemporary composers such as Aaron Copland, *El Salon Mexico*; silence, *Drama of Motion*; a Metropolitan Opera production of Schoenberg; and choreography for plays, such as Molière's *School for Wives*.

Humphrey's technique and her concepts of how to choreograph have survived more than her pieces, however. She experimented with the concept of balance, most especially, fall and recovery. Believing that dance existed on "the arc between two deaths," her choreography emphasized the muscular drama inherent in balance and imbalance, the contrasts between giving way to gravity altogether and resisting gravity to regain equilibrium. Examples of Humphrey technique can be seen today in almost any modern dance concert in which dancers fall to the ground and then spring back, or swing in one direction and then pendulum back to the other, making arcs with arms, torso, and body. She taught at Bennington College, and she wrote *The Art of Making Dances*, which became the definitive handbook for dance composition.

When the Humphrey/Weidman company disbanded in 1945, **Charles Weidman** (1901–1975) worked on Broadway and founded his own school and company, as well as choreographing for New York City Opera and various theater productions. He established the Expression of Two Arts Theatre in New York with the sculptor Mikhail Santaro in the early sixties and, like many of the pioneer modern dancers, continued to perform right up to his death in 1975.

Weidman is known for the satirical vein that runs through his works, such as *And Daddy Was a Fireman, A House Divided, Fables for Our Time, The War Between Men and Women,* and *Is Sex Necessary?* His choreography, which used pantomime, gesture, and spoofs on old silent films, provided a much needed contrast to the overbearing dramatic and emotional works of the earlier pioneers. Proof of Weidman's break from the traditions into which the modern dance revolt was becoming ensconced, is the fact that, instead of creating more modern dance companies, Weidman's most influential pupils, **Jack Cole** and **Bob Fosse**, went on to choreograph for Broadway.

Meanwhile, **Doris Humphrey** did something unusual in the trend of modern dance by becoming the artistic director of a company *other* than her own—the José Limón Company. **Limón** (1908–1972), had danced with Humphrey's troupe from 1930 to 1940. His leave-taking was rare for being amicable. Thus did teacher join pupil, continuing to choreograph along with Limón, who is best remembered for *The Moor's Pavane*. This encapsulated version of *Othello*, in which the emotional drama between four characters erupts within the confines of the formal *pavane*, or court dance, has been mounted on numerous ballet companies, most notably the Joffrey, and performed by **Nureyev** on United States tours.

Limón's work is characterized by its dramatic content and impact, often based upon story or legend. Though originally trained in Humphrey technique, Limón evolved his own style, which matches gesture to choreographic intent. After his death, his company was at first run cooperatively and then continued under the directorship of **Ruth Currier**, who was one of his primary soloists (along with **Pauline Koner**, **Betty Jones**, and **Lucas Hoving**). The Limón company was unusual in that it survived the death of its artistic director. (The Humphrey, Weidman, and Shawn dance companies all folded.)

The tendency in the modern dance movement, from Denishawn forward, was to take the dance technique and choreographic style of the company one performed with and then found one's own company in a manner that either expanded upon those principles (José Limón) or reacted against them (Martha Graham).

Martha Graham, who was born in 1894, danced with Denishawn from 1916 to 1923. While Denishawn gave her background training, she felt its dance pageants to be too stilted and not at all connected with human emotions. A rebel and iconoclast from the beginning, Graham began choreographing solos on a freelance basis before founding her own company (in 1927), as well as the Martha Graham School of Contemporary Dance, which offered specific training in "Graham technique."

Graham's compact body was the basis for creating her early choreography, which was extremely serious as compared with the entertaining spectacles of Denishawn. And, unlike Doris Humphrey's emotional conflicts, Graham explored movement as an expression of psychological drama. Her "ballets," as she called them, were usually stories about heroic women in myths and history, with herself in the leading role.

Graham's work also was characterized by its use of costumes, props, and set design integral to the action. She collaborated with the artist Isamu Noguchi and later with the designer Halston. Fabric was an important element in her dances, especially long gowns that wound around the dancer's legs as they turned, encompassing or entrapping them. (The tight, stretchable robe inside of which the solo *Lamentation* takes place becomes a symbol of the isolation caused by grief.) Her dancers often wear large headdresses or masks. Sometimes a dancer wraps around a sculpture, sinuous and seductive; or mounts the sections of set to indicate power and control. Portions of the set also come apart to become symbolic props for the dancers to carry.

While she returned to the past for her dance themes, Graham's music was usually the product of a collaboration with contemporary composers. She worked also in association with her music teacher, Louis Horst (1884–1964), who had previously collaborated with **Ruth St. Denis**. Horst composed several of Graham's ballets, as well as teaching dance composition and authoring two books, *Pre-Classic Dance Forms* and *Modern Dance Forms in Relation to the Other Modern Arts*.

Like most modern dancers, past and present, Graham invented her technique as she went along. She is most famous for the creation of "contraction and release," based upon exaggerations of breathing. Instead of concealing effort the way ballet does, Graham revealed it as a true aspect of life. A percussive style enabled her to depict emotional extremes and, since the 1940s, Graham choreographed dance dramas depicting figures from history, literature, and mythology with characters symbolic of universal psychological traits.

"The primary bond between people is undoubtedly physical, since the body is the one thing we all have in common. . . . The function of dance is communication. . . . By communication is not meant to tell a story or to project an idea, but to communicate experience by means of action and perceived by action. . . . This is the reason for the appearance of modern dance. The departure of the dance from classical and romantic delineations was not an end in itself, but the means to an end. It was not done perversely to dramatize ugliness, or to strike at sacred tradition—to destroy from sheer inability to become proficient in the technical demands of a classical art. The old forms could not give voice to the more fully awakened man." Thus does the articulate Martha Graham explain why not only she, but those who follow her, choreograph as they do.

Graham's most influential student is **Merce Cunningham** (b. 1919). After performing with Graham from 1939 to 1945, Cunningham began his own company in 1953, along with an entirely new dance technique. Cunningham presents pure movement—sometimes based on the everyday, like people walking down the street. The dance's meaning comes from how the viewer chooses to interpret it. The concept of mixing the elements of music, set, costumes, and dance into a cohesive whole was shifted into a new relationship of all the theatrical elements, in which each is its own center, not requiring the support of the others.

His dancers do not use the rhythmic beat of the musical compositions as a basis for their movement, since Cunningham felt the dancing itself to have its own rhythm. His dances contain very slow *adagio* sections, in which his dancers hold poses or balances endlessly, contrasted with drastic tempo changes to technically difficult *allegro* movements, tremendously quick, and demanding virtuosity on the part of the dancers. (To be a member of his company is an honor in the modern dance world similar to joining the New York City Ballet and indeed, Cunningham and **Balanchine** have in common their insistence on the primacy of the dancing itself.)

Several different sections are performed onstage at one time without the need to be either related or synchronized. A solo may be downstage, while a duet is finishing upstage, while a small ensemble is entering with unison movement. Thus making every area of the stage a focal point, Cunningham requires decision-making on the part of the audience as to what to watch amidst dancing that is happening simultaneously.

Paul Taylor, born in 1930, also performed with Cunningham and Graham. When he founded his own company in 1954, Taylor had developed a style like neither of his mentors. Taylor's choreography is light (as opposed to Graham's drama), often humorous, and definitely aligned to the music (unlike Cunningham). Taylor uses baroque and classic composers, such as Haydn, Vivaldi, and Bach; but his choreography does not match the music, in that the movement is not classical in form.

His style includes very rounded arms, *demi-pliés* with the working foot pointed against the lower calf and ankle of the supporting leg, and a high technical demand on his dancers. Another Taylor thematic movement is quick, low *jetés* across

the stage, usually performed by the men. Most of his choreography was created on his own body and continues to be
performed by lead males (in contrast to Graham) who tend
to have similar body builds to Taylor. Like Graham and Cunningham, Taylor created his own movement style and technique for training dancers.

These three are nearly as "classical" today as ballet in that
their styles are formulated, their technique codified, and their
choreography indicative of their particular vision of modern
dance. Their repertory has been repeated and revised for at
least three decades so that some of their works have become
standard, much like ballets.

Unusual in that his influence may have been as much in
his teaching as in his choreography, was **Lester Horton**
(1906–1953). Although he began by studying ballet with
Adolph Bolm, Horton was also influenced by Japanese and
American Indian dances. The Lester Horton Dancers, founded
in 1934 in Los Angeles, produced not only his choreography
but also such future choreographers as Bella Lewitzky (whose
company is still based in Los Angeles) and Alvin Ailey.

In addition to performing with Horton's company—becoming director when Horton died in 1953—**Ailey** (1931–89)
studied with Graham, Holm, and Weidman. He also studied
ballet and acting and appeared in musicals, films, and plays.
His creation of the Alvin Ailey American Dance Theater
resulted in a multiracial troupe known especially for those
works such as *Revelations* (set to Negro spirituals) and *Blues
Suite* (set to familiar Southern blues songs), which comment
upon the black experience in America.

A dancer whose company crosses the border between ballet
and modern dance is **Arthur Mitchell** (b. 1934). Originally
a principal dancer with the New York City Ballet, Mitchell
left that company upon the assassination of Martin Luther
King, returned to Harlem, and started a school for dance there,

which grew into the Dance Theater of Harlem (known as DTH). While Mitchell at first wanted to prove that black bodies could perform classical ballet (he had been one of the only black dancers in a ballet company), his troupe also performs jazz, ethnic, and modern dance, in everything from full-length classics (such as their Creole version of *Giselle*, set in New Orleans) to pieces representative of black life, choreographed to contemporary composers.

An iconoclast who became standard through longevity is **Alwin Nikolais** (b. 1912). Nik (as he is called) studied with Graham, Humphrey/Weidman, and Hanya Holm before becoming Holm's assistant. Today it's not so easy to see this background influence in his work because Nik turned to a new use for movement—experimental theater.

When he became director of New York's Henry Street Playhouse in 1948, Nik reorganized the school and performing company while developing his concept of a new dance theater in which the dancer provides the kinetic energy for a stage play consisting of abstract forms, patterns, colors, and sounds. These elements are closely integrated (the polar opposite of Cunningham), with Nikolais himself serving as author, director, choreographer, composer, designer, and lighting director.

He has described these almost one-man productions as "sound and vision pieces," and their titles are indicative of the nonhuman nature of the movement: *Masks, Props and Mobiles, Kaleidoscope, Structures, Cross-Fade*. Nik's pieces, which seem to draw more inspiration from his days as a puppet master, are a visual and aural delight with dancers inside structures or unpredictable costumes that conjure images of animals, aliens, and machines. The movement tends toward repeated phrases, and often the body parts are segmented, with only feet protruding from the set structure, or hands in white gloves black-lit so as to appear floating in space.

Nikolais' collaborator, until he struck off on his own in the mid-fifties, was **Murray Louis** (b. 1926). Louis had a vision of dance quite different from Nikolais, although their two companies continued to share the same building. Louis's choreography returned to the pure technical dance idiom with a skillful dash of wit thrown in. It is quick, kinetic, and—perhaps its only similarity to Nik—separates body parts, focusing on how each looks when moving in isolation from the others.

One of the most notable examples of the latter was a solo Louis premiered in 1984, *Frail Demons*, in which his extraordinary body disjointed itself in an endless variety of improbable and entertaining ways. Louis has also performed in collaboration with the Dave Brubeck trio, using choreography that —similar to ballet—astonishes with one amazing solo after another, each one displaying specific qualities of his dancers.

The creation of these dissimilar new styles, along with "classic" teaching techniques, did not stop the evolution of modern dance. The concept of what dance is keeps expanding as modern dancers encourage innovation.

In the early sixties, the **Judson Dance Theater** culled a group of performers, including artists, composers, writers, and dancers, who challenged the very definitions of dance. For them, modern dance had become stagnant; the major modern dancers were either emulated or rebelled against, but little was truly new. The artists involved in the Judson Theater believed that dance could be removed from a theater setting, and that it required no specific technique, training, or equipment. No compositional formula was used by this group either, which originally performed in the Greenwich Village church from which it got its name, and later in art galleries, lofts, and other nonproscenium spaces. Not always technically trained, these dancers often wore street shoes, the forerunner of the sneakers that later became almost the hallmark of "post-modern" dancers.

This challenge was matched on the West Coast by **Anna Halprin** (b. 1920), who offered movement workshops specifically for nondancers. Her workshop participants performed, in a natural environment, theater pieces that were expressions of inner discovery, created through a group process. These segued into dances performed in various sections of the city of San Francisco, by people "off the street" with no dance training, and—finally—to her annual Circle the Earth celebration, which is performed by hundreds of people simultaneously in various parts of the world, after participation in an intensive workshop.

Along the modern dance timeline came **Twyla Tharp** (b. 1942), who had a sort of "classical" modern dance education by studying with Graham and Cunningham and performing with Paul Taylor from 1963 to 1965. With a similar stubbornness of vision, Tharp created myriad experimental works before arriving at her own concept of choreography. Her distinctive style was recognizable, almost immediately, as unique. While Tharp's choreography evolved into a new style of modern dance, it also became a comment upon dance itself.

Tharp's quirky, unusual movement allows her to poke fun at standard dance steps, often getting rid of them completely or performing them wrong on purpose. (She does this especially with the ballet idiom, at which she is adept.) Tharp uses all the existing forms—including ballet, jazz, and tap—to create a new way of looking that reminds the viewer of their commonality—dance. In this vein, Tharp believes that there should be no distinctions between ballet and modern.

Tharp required her troupe to wear jazz shoes because of the speed her choreography demands. (Bare feet tend to stick to the stage, especially during turns.) She hired dancers trained in ballet for their greater technical facility, and dancers from ballet companies have been known to "defect" to her company.

Ballet dancers can get bored with standard repertory. On the whole, modern dance companies premiere more new works every year than ballet companies do.

Tharp's choice of music is fairly atypical as well. She has used popular songs by the Beach Boys, Jerome Kern, or Jelly Roll Morton, as well as working with contemporary composers such as Philip Glass, and using a Haydn symphony for an ABT-commissioned ballet. From early obscure days with a small company barely surviving, Tharp gained a reputation as a choreographer, first for Joffrey, then for American Ballet Theatre, where she became artistic associate in 1988. She also choreographed four feature films: *Hair, Ragtime, Amadeus,* and *White Nights.*

Minimalism pared dance down to its basics. **Trisha Brown** (b. 1936) choreographed through repetition—her pieces were performed like a musical "canon": one dancer began a movement phrase, the second dancer repeated that phrase and added another, and so on. Works were sometimes presented outside, with dancers quite a distance apart, within just enough range to watch and repeat the next phrase, as across rooftops in the city of New York. Brown herself performed *accumulated* phrases, with slight variation, ad infinitum, often accompanied by spoken monologues. Brown's work continues to evolve, including collaborating with Robert Rauschenberg, but primarily her choreography is characterized by everyday, almost casual-looking kinetic/frenetic movement.

Although she originally studied ballet, Cunningham and Graham techniques, **Meredith Monk** (b. 1942) created elaborate theater pieces—as much drama as dance—which combined movement, metaphor, and symbolism with her own music. Monk's musical compositions have been recognized to the point that she has performed them in concerts separate from her dances. As an "instrument," her voice evokes primal, tribal, and primitive memories and emotions—often making use of the concept of repetition, as in a religious chant.

One of Monk's most talked about pieces was *Vessel*, which was performed in three different locations in New York City, the audience being bused from place to place for each part. Like many of her cohorts, Monk also presented pieces in her own loft—a space to which her unusual angle on dance presentation was well adapted, as she put the audience in the performing area and the dancers in the living space.

Films, which she produced in collaboration with Ping Chong, combined vocalizations, music, narrative, and dance for a type of theater not unlike that of Robert Wilson (*Einstein on the Beach*) in its epic proportions and tedious length, meant to challenge the audience's concept of time, space, and what theater/dance should be. Monk's legacy today is probably the performance artist, who combines all the arts to create pieces that use movement in conjunction with other theatrical elements.

Laura Dean (b. 1945) danced with Meredith Monk and Paul Taylor, and studied with Lucas Hoving (lead dancer with José Limón) and Merce Cunningham. Her background is indeed a synthesis of the history of modern dance, a history available today to all future modern dance choreographers. (The modern dance norm has become to study several styles —from the masters to the innovators—perform with several quite different companies, and, finally, to arrive at a unique style for oneself and then go out and establish a company to perform it.)

Dean reduced dance to repeatable phrases, which gain intensity from their very redundancy. She also invented a phenomenal method of spinning in which the dancer does not spot.

In ballet, SPOTTING was created to help a dancer maintain equilibrium while turning. Spotting consists of keeping the eyes riveted on one spot, whipping the head around with each body revolution to that same focus. Spotting is how dancers are able to stop so quickly without being dizzy after a series of turns.

When Dean's dancers turn, their focus remains frontal, in the same direction the body is going, the gaze so bland as to make the dancers appear mesmerized. These spins are repeated endlessly, like a mantra, and with the same hypnotic effect. The impact of a stage crowded with dancers spinning endlessly in their individual worlds, yet never bumping into one another is extraordinarily compelling.

Like the spinning, the rest of Dean's choreography also uses this repetitive technique, with a phrase made up of a few steps repeated by one line of dancers moving to the front of the stage, then another line, then another, and then the first again. When that theme has been repeated to the point of highest tension, the dancers shift to another theme and begin repeating that, over and over.

Dean has gained some popularity outside her own dance company with the works she has been commissioned to create on the Joffrey Ballet, proving that rebels can cross the line into the classical tradition—and, that classically trained ballet dancers are perfectly capable of executing the exigencies of modern dance.

To add to the confusion of defining modern dance, the term POST-MODERN DANCE was coined in the late sixties. This term is sometimes used to include everyone choreographing after Judson. Like the delineations between ballet and modern dance, definitions of words such as "post-modern" and "avant-garde" befuddle both artist and spectator. More important than categorizing each genre is learning and accepting the choreography for how it looks. Post-modern, Judson, or avant-garde choreographers don't need specific titles so much as recognition for their contributions to new ways of moving—and therefore looking at, dance.

On the whole, these choreographers have questioned the fact that modern dance has become too standardized in its techniques and too classical in performance style. The techniques of Cunningham, Graham, Holm, Limón, and Taylor are prescribed to the point that they can be taught all over the world—and are. Returning to the original tenets of Isadora, post-moderns feel that dance should always be breaking new ground, defying the rules of dance, performance, and even steps. For them, refining technique is less crucial than composing dances that are comprised of normal behavior rather than extraordinary steps.

David Gordon (b. 1936), for instance, performs pieces that look as if the dancers are not "dancing," in the definition of the term audiences have come to expect. His choreography is often based on casual or everyday movement—so ordinary, in fact, that it appears offhand or improvised and is therefore astounding when the dancers repeat the same sequence of actions exactly the same way. While his dancers are highly trained technically, the sort of display of difficult "steps" that so amaze dance audiences does not show up in his works. Movement is instead incomplete, or unexpected, such as an *arabesque* that is just about to stretch full out only to become instead a limp leg with a shrug of the shoulders.

Over the years, the tendency for dancer/choreographers to leave a company after a certain number of performing years to found a company and a school for their own technique has changed. More often, instead of starting a school along with their company, many modern choreographers today just create dances in their particular style and expect their company members to train elsewhere. This training will most likely include both ballet and some classical modern dance form, i.e., Cunningham, Graham, Holm, Limón, Taylor.

Also, a choreographer's purpose is not to create a technique, but to create dances. In the early days of modern dance, a choreographer had to create a technique in order for his dancers to perform the new kind of movement. Requirements for the body were different for each new type of choreography. Sufficient variety in technique classes exists today so that dancers arrive as perfect putty for a choreographer, well versed in many styles and therefore technically capable of doing anything the choreographer might ask. Now choreographers who break off from a company to begin creating dances focus on doing just that—choreographing, not training dancers.

These choreographers quite often do not establish companies on their own immediately. Pick-up companies, comprised of dancers interested in working with that particular choreographer, may stay together just for one performance "set" or come back together whenever that choreographer gets another performance "gig." Early in a career, choreographers may not have the resources to keep dancers employed year-round. Sometimes they struggle to find studio space in which to create and affordable theaters in which to perform.

These factors have resulted in another interesting phenomenon for modern dancers: quite often, dancers appear with two or more troupes simultaneously. With great agility, they juggle performing seasons and rehearsal schedules. What this provides, however, is full-time employment for the dancer who might not otherwise dance that frequently. Smaller companies may perform only once or twice a year, with a mere three to five performances per gig.

Most choreographers, however, want a troupe of dancers

who remain stable. (Company rosters have been known to change every season, as modern dancers try out other troupes.) In the more well-known modern companies of Alvin Ailey, Merce Cunningham, Martha Graham, Alwin Nikolais, Paul Taylor, dancers may stay for most of their career, in similar fashion to the way ballet dancers join one ballet company.

Choreography may be modified by new dancers or as the choreographer is inspired by the way new dancers move. This change in company composition has always characterized modern much more than ballet, as modern dancers feel free to switch to other choreography or to experiment with the different styles of modern dance. After all, modern dance as a philosophy *encourages* creativity.

From Isadora to the present, tenets of modern dance have been created that serve, in an historical context, to distinguish it from ballet. The most obvious is that the dancing is bare footed with legs and feet parallel instead of turned out. And the ground—or various horizontal positions upon the stage—is considered as viable a space for dancing as is the air, or various combinations of vertical.

The bare foot is both unhampered by the *pointe* shoe and freer to contact the ground. This allows a sense of being closer to the earth. Balance is surer and the dancer does not have to go through the machinations necessary to ballet—rosin, preparation of the *pointe* shoe, breaking in the shoe, etcetera—that, to the modern dancer's viewpoint, seem unnatural artifice. The bare foot is also symbolic of the human body unadorned, without anything added to make it look better than it is.

Modern dancers present the body in what they believe to be a more natural form, without the attempt to make it appear perfect, which is the grand illusion of ballet. Removing the stiff bodice of the tutu from women and the tight jacket from the men, modern dancers began experimenting with a fluid, loose torso instead of the erect posture required by ballet. First performing in tunics and gowns and flowing robes, these experimenters later danced in the leotard. It was similar to a second skin and allowed the human body to be as free as when naked. The consequent mobility resulted in technique changes.

The leotard, a stretch tunic covering the torso, has become standard practice wear only since 1948. Its development goes back to the early nineteenth century when a costume and hose maker for the Paris Opéra, named Maillot, made knitted, close-fitting dance wear known as "fleshings." Later in that same century the trapeze artist *Jules Léotard* outfitted himself in fleshings from tip to toe, transforming them into costume with embroidery and decoration.

Doris Humphrey's "fall and recovery" was illustrative of modern dance's use of gravity and, consequently, the floor. Often, modern technique classes are taught on the floor, as opposed to ballet classes, in which students stand either at the *barre* or in the center of the studio. (Modern dancer **Merce Cunningham**, however, teaches his entire company class standing, saying something like, "Since we are going to be dancing on our feet, that's how we'll take class.") Choreographically, the floor is considered to be another aspect of space, with a dramatic focus on "down," while ballet tends to emphasize "up," with *pointe* shoes being the penultimate in attempts to get off, or away from, the ground. Ballet defies gravity; modern dance works with it.

In Merce Cunningham technique, the back is elongated right up to the tip of the spine in the base of the skull, so that any forward bend appears to be much longer than the same movement would in ballet. **Martha Graham** is perhaps most famous for the creation of the "contraction." This movement originates in the solar plexus, as a deep sucking in—as if one were just socked in the belly. When executed correctly, this contraction will ripple out from the solar plexus, affecting the rest of the torso and spine.

Modern also uses the head and neck in a less rigid fashion than ballet. Every possible variety and combination of positioning the neck has been used in modern dance choreography. (Remember the *technique* was developed so that dancers could execute the *choreography*.) In ballet, on the other hand, the head, neck, and shoulders are aligned in specific ways that are strictly—and often rigidly—adhered to for correct classical form.

In similar fashion, ballet is presented primarily on the frontal axis. The various directional positions of the body—*écarté* ("wide apart," at oblique angle to audience), *croisé* (working leg crosses line of body), *effacé* ("obscured," body partly hidden from audience), *de face* (facing straight forward toward the audience)—all maintain a forward presentation of the body toward the audience. In modern dance, anything may be seen, from direct side views (like figures on a Greek vase), to having the back to the audience. Closed (such as parallel feet or folded arms) positions, as well as open (turned out feet, extended arms) are employed choreographically.

The stage picture is also used differently in modern dance. The hierarchy of classical ballet is discarded. No longer is there a line of *corps de ballet* in the back with soloists in front. Each section of the stage is considered equally important and several solos may be performed simultaneously.

These changes in the format of choreography and staging hierarchy for the dancers were the result of another major difference between classical ballet and classical modern dance—equality among the dancers. Often each modern dancer is a soloist, therefore no one appears in a subordinate position onstage. While some may stand out as having the principal roles in, for instance, Martha Graham ballets, in most modern dance companies each dancer performs a solo at some time, either within the same dance or in other repertory at the same performance.

Another difference choreographically is that modern dance companies usually perform three distinct works in a performance—more like the mixed-bill evening of ballet than the full-length or story ballet. And while the choreography for all pieces in a program is usually executed entirely by the company's artistic director, and therefore similar stylistically, it may vary in tone from somber to witty, or in configuration from large ensemble to a few soloists. A ballet company, on the other hand, may present works from three different choreographers in the same evening.

The parallel positions of modern dance were a direct result of modern dance's genesis—a revolt against the unnaturalness of ballet. Turnout is hard on the hips and knees—and, according to early modern dance pioneers, not the way human beings naturally move. But modern had an entire vocabulary preceding it. Not to throw out the baby with the bath water, most modern technique classes include both turned out and parallel exercises. Modern dance has borrowed steps from ballet and often even uses the same French names for them. But where modern technique uses ballet steps, it either expands upon them to include everyday and pedestrian movement or elaborates and modifies the step. What is wrong technically in ballet may be intentional in modern.

The flexed foot is another creation of modern dance. Instead of pointing the toes all the time to make a perfect line through space, modern choreography often cuts that look with the extended foot remaining flexed, as if flat on the floor. This position, like most of modern dance technique, evolved from the choreographic need to express genuine feelings and show the human body in what was believed to be a more honest way.

Early modern dance pioneers, especially Martha Graham, claimed that human beings are not always beautiful; nor does the body always look perfect. Their choreography sought to expose the human body in a more natural way from ballet, which meant including these less perfect aspects.

Along these lines, modern dance choreographers also sought greater latitude with regard to subject matter. Up to the time of the modern dance revolution, most ballet tended to focus on beauty, with fairy tales and supernatural spirits from the Romantic age. While choreographers during Diaghilev's day had made overtures toward expressing contemporary life, ballet was primarily premised upon the more positive, pure, or perfect aspects of life. Not exactly an honest portrayal of everyday life, ballet was more often an escape from it.

Modern dance pioneers wanted to express how they really felt—about everything. **Martha Graham**'s famous solo *Lamentation* dealt with how the human body expresses grief. Not one word was needed for the audience to be moved to tears from the suffering contained, exposed, and then nearly screamed through body movements by the soloist.

Although **Isadora** was concerned with movement that would convey how music made her feel, she also explored specific emotions, such as nurturing and letting go in her solo *Mother*. Other choreographers after her also experimented with music that had not previously been considered appropriate for dancing. **Ted Shawn**'s male dancers, for instance, performed to percussion; his wife, **Ruth St. Denis**, used East Indian music and was influenced choreographically by Egyptian and Oriental designs and art. One of Humphrey's more remembered works was *Air on a G String*, originally choreographed to be a "visual" advertisement for the first recording of that Bach composition. **Paul Taylor** also choreographed to Bach, Handel, Haydn, as well as contemporary composers.

Martha Graham and **Merce Cunningham** commissioned compositions specifically for their choreography. Graham worked closely with her composers so that both choreography and music were created with the other in mind. But, while music commissioned for Merce Cunningham is often composed simultaneously with the choreography, Cunningham himself may not even hear it until the premiere performance. He revolutionized the concept of what a dance performance should be by suggesting that the various elements—music, dance, scene design—are not interdependent, or even related, except to occur at the same time during a performance. While studying at the Cornish School of Fine Arts in Seattle, Cunningham met John Cage, who became his musical collaborator and who introduced him to the use of chance operations as a method of making creative decisions.

Cunningham and Cage believe that dance and music are not interdependent; they simply are performed at the same time and in the same place "for audience convenience," Cage once explained. Cunningham has commissioned scores by Cage, David Tudor, and Takahisa Kosugi, among others, continuing his reputation for remaining in the forefront of music as he always has in design, with sets and costumes (also considered independent of the choreography) by such famous artists as Jasper Johns, Andy Warhol, and Robert Rauschenberg.

George Balanchine had a longtime association with Igor Stravinsky and also choreographed to composers not generally associated with ballet, such as George Gershwin, Richard Rodgers, and John Philip Sousa. In 1959, he choreographed *Episodes* with Martha Graham. Originally a close collaboration between the two was envisioned, but later it was decided to divide the ballet into two sections: Graham choreographed the first half which used dancers from her own company, plus ballerina **Sallie Wilson**. Graham's segment, true to her choreographic vision, was a story with a plot. The second half of the ballet was Balanchine's choreography, without narrative, and performed by members of his company, plus Graham's dancer, **Paul Taylor**.

On the flip side, there have been many instances of modern dance choreographers setting pieces on ballet companies: **Lar Lubovitch** for New York City Ballet; **Twyla Tharp** for Joffrey, ABT, and NYCB; **Laura Dean** for Joffrey; **Mark Morris** for ABT. Pieces by Cunningham appear in the repertory of several ballet companies. Tharp also choreographed her original *Deuce Coupe* in 1973 for members of the Joffrey Ballet *and* her own company. The dance was divided by costume and style into modern and ballet, with Tharp's company dancing the modern and Joffrey's the ballet. In spite of this separation, *Deuce Coupe* provided an interesting platform for the synthesis of the two styles. And, it became so popular that Tharp later revised the choreography for the Joffrey Ballet to perform alone, *Deuce Coupe II*, giving those dancers an opportunity to dance her modern technique.

Some ballet dancers have successfully segued into modern dance as a career transition: **Nureyev** danced with Martha Graham and Paul Taylor; both Joffrey and ABT dancers have joined Twyla Tharp's company. Many dancers take classes in both ballet and modern in order to develop a sound basic technique. Dancers are being required, more and more, to be facile in both techniques.

For the most part, however, dancers train initially in ballet because it is still a codified system that prepares the body in a carefully regimented, graded fashion. Ballet dancers are still generally considered to be more technical than modern dancers; it is usually easier for a ballet dancer to dance modern choreography than for a member of a modern dance troupe to join a ballet company. (This was aptly illustrated when Twyla Tharp brought seven dancers from her own company with her to American Ballet Theatre and artistic director Baryshnikov was quoted as saying, "I'll use them as much as I can, but I'm not going to put them in toe shoes in the front line of *Swan Lake*.")

In terms of their career, most dancers still consider themselves to be either ballet or modern. In that sense, the term "modern" is still a good division. Many modern dance techniques incorporate the codified vocabulary of ballet, both in class and choreography, partly because those terms are universally recognized to describe a certain dance step. Where modern differs is in its expansion of that vocabulary to include steps that may have no name, or are casual on-the-street movements. **Lucas Hoving**, for instance, uses only ballet names for steps when he teaches; **Merce Cunningham**, on the other hand, demonstrates the steps, describing them verbally ("jump," "brush"), without using any French terms except *plié* and *relevé*.

The blurring of the line between the two schools is, finally, exemplified in the fact that the term modern dance has lost its specific meaning over the years. There is now modern ballet, contemporary ballet, and a host of other terms (neo-classicism, psychological ballet, dance dramas, and so on) that were devised in order to identify styles and variations, but actually have only clouded the issue.

Most of this chapter pertains to the historical development of modern dance, for many of the modern elements—especially use of the floor, emotional verisimilitude, freer costumes—have been incorporated into the ballet world. But modern dance will still generally include these elements, while ballet is still the "classical" form handed down since the time of Louis XIV, with *pointe* shoes, tutus, turnout, and a host of steps named in French. That's simplification for the sake of being able to discuss what's seen onstage.

And, after all, that's what both forms are about—dancing.

DANCERS

Dance Steps

Dance requires a style, or a look, which generally consists of straight knees, a pulled up back, an erect head, and an upright torso. This carriage is maintained throughout whatever dance movement is being performed. Correct execution of any step always includes proper alignment of the body.

Alignment has to do with the line the dancing body inscribes in space. A dancer's LINE is defined by keeping the head, shoulders, torso, hips, knees, and toes in sequence one with another. The body should therefore appear to move as if it is a connected unit, creating a long continuous line in space uninterrupted by joints.

In ballet, this projection of a beautiful line is the primary intent. A classical dancer is judged by the purity of that line and its accord with the rigid prescriptions of the tradition.

A dancer should not break the continuous line of the body down through the leg to the extended toes (unless a flexed foot is specifically indicated by the choreography). While the FLEXED look—the foot at a 90-degree angle to the calf, as when standing on the floor—was created by modern dance and now is used in contemporary ballet choreography as well, it looks quite different from a failure to point the entire foot. The former is a specific dramatic look, the latter is sloppy dancing. However, keeping the toes pointed while moving is difficult, especially when getting on and off the ground quickly, which requires going from a flexed foot to a fully pointed foot in the air.

Another element of alignment is *épaulement* (shouldering), a term used in ballet to describe the way shoulder, neck, and head positions correspond. (Primary ingredients are *croisé*, or crossed, and *effacé*, open.) PORT DE BRAS, or carriage of the arms, refers not only to the positioning of the arms but also how they look. *Port de bras* for the arms is practiced in class in addition to leg exercises.

No matter how the arms, wrists, and hands are positioned, they must look lovely, giving the impression of effortless movement while floating through space. The fingers are the final extension of the picture the body makes moving through space and as such are the last statement—they should be neither overly curved (as if curling back in toward the palms) or overly straight, as if pointing the finger at someone. Wrists must never go limp, letting the hands droop below the level of the forearm, nor should the elbows drop, making fore and upper arm angular to one another. Likewise, a dancer's arms should not become rigid during the execution of difficult steps using the feet and legs. Sometimes the fingers will straighten too much with the effort of a lift, as if the dancer is fearful, or trying too hard.

The upper arm, elbow, forearm, wrist, and fingers should extend out from one another in an elongated, slightly rounded, look. The exception to this basic rule for dance would be intentional angularity or a breaking of the continuous line from shoulder to fingers, for dramatic effect. (Again, this is most likely to occur in modern dance choreography.)

Finally, alignment is affected by TURNOUT, an outward rotation of the legs beginning from the hip through the thigh and knee down to the feet, which then face away from each other. Although modern dance, and some contemporary ballet choreography, may use intentional parallel positioning of the feet and legs, nearly all forms of dance use turnout at some time.

In lieu of the parallel position in which most of us walk, turnout was developed in the early 1700s to facilitate technical virtuosity. Correct turnout is essential to proper execution of most dance steps, since it enables the entire leg to move more freely. Pointing the toes of the feet away from each other also provides a more stable base of support from which to begin difficult maneuvers. When the feet are turned out, the legs are ready to move in any direction.

To experience turnout, stand with feet and legs together, toes facing in front of you, as if you were about to walk forward. Shifting the weight onto your heels, lift the balls of the feet off the floor and place the toes away from each other. A perfect turnout would be 180 degrees described by the feet. While turnout may seem quite awkward at first, for professional dancers it is more comfortable than standing with legs and feet parallel.

Dancers learn turnout by starting with toes pointed slightly away from each other, gradually increasing the turned-out position with daily practice. Trying to turn out too drastically right away cannot only injure the knees—on which turnout exerts a lot of pressure—but also adversely affect the alignment of the entire body. The trick is to turn the feet out as far as possible without disturbing this line. Turning out beyond a dancer's technical range will distort the rest of the body, especially the back, or the legs when they are raised from the ground.

The following **five basic positions** (all of which illustrate turnout), define the beginning and end of any movement, serve as preparation for more complicated steps, and are used as transitions between moves. They alternate between closed and open placement of the feet, i.e., first position is closed, second is open, etc. During a performance, one position will meld into another, so that the basic steps seem difficult to separate, but do watch for them. With time they'll be more easily discerned.

FIRST POSITION: The heels are brought together, with the feet rotated so that the toes point away from each other.

SECOND POSITION: The right foot is moved away from the left in the direction of the right toes, until the feet are straight apart, making a wider base of support.

THIRD POSITION: The right foot is brought back in toward the left until the heel is fitting snugly against the arch of the left foot. (This position is rarely used.)

FOURTH POSITION: The right foot is placed straight forward until the heel of the right foot lines up with the big toe joint of the left. (Now the space extends from front to back instead of side to side, as in second position.)

FIFTH POSITION: The right foot is brought back toward the left until the right heel is against either the base of the big toe or entirely crossed, against the end of the big toe of the left foot (depending upon the school: French, Italian, Russian). Toes should be pointing away from each other; thighs, knees, calves together.

There are corresponding **positions of the arms** as well, but they vary according to the school, such as Vaganova, Cecchetti, Royal Academy of Dancing, School of American Ballet. Indeed, the differences from studio to studio are most pronounced in America. (This is one reason why most teachers believe in always demonstrating the arms, as their look—and not their name—is what matters.) The same location of the arms may be referred to with different names. For instance, "first position" is called "preparation" in some schools and "fifth position *en bas*" in others.

The third and fourth positions of the arms have the greatest variety; the illustrations here are of one form only (most often referred to as French) and are not meant to represent the definitive third or fourth position for all systems of classic dance (which are usually classed into three—French, Italian, or Russian).

Remember, also, that a position of the "arms" refers to everything from the neck to the tip of the fingers, since the impression should be of a continuous line.

FIRST POSITION: The arms are rounded down, fingertips toward one another. (In the school that calls this position PREPARATION, first position would be: arms are rounded frontward chest height, palms facing the chest, fingers almost touching, tips toward one another.)

SECOND POSITION: Each arm is extended directly to the side of the body, parallel to the floor, slightly forward of the shoulders.

THIRD POSITION: One arm is positioned over the head, the other extended out to the side, as in second position.

FOURTH POSITION: One arm is placed to the side, the other rounded in front of the chest.

FIFTH POSITION: Both arms are raised overhead, forming a circle; the dancer should be able to see the palms with her eyes, without lifting the head. Also *en bas*, same position but arms are down.

While arms and feet are both designated by number in the basic positions, and many a beginning student of dance can illustrate these in order, they are not necessarily performed together. In other words, it is possible in the middle of a choreographic step for a dancer's feet to be in fourth position while the arms are in fifth.

Learning ballet vocabulary consists of matching French words to athletic accomplishments. Remember, ballet steps were developed from court dances of the French nobility and the first dance school to codify and name the steps was in Paris. Within the huge vocabulary of dance steps, most can be divided into two categories: ALLEGRO, or those performed quickly, to a fast tempo; and ADAGIO, or those performed slowly. (These are not hard and fast delineations, but it helps to separate the two while learning the names of steps.) The CENTER WORK—or that done after exercises at the barre in the middle of the studio—of every ballet class is also divided into *allegro* and *adagio*.

Most forms of *allegro* fall into two categories: **batterie** (beats), which are steps done off the ground, requiring some form of BEATING, or touching the legs and feet together while in the air; and **jeté** (throw), which refers to leaps. Both *batterie* and *jetés* require ÉLÉVATION, or the ability to get up into the air (*en l'air*). All these maneuvers require sufficient elevation in order to be completed fully before the feet touch the ground again.

In order to get up into the air, dancers **plié** (bend). This step is seen quite frequently onstage, and is actually a **demi-plié**, or half bend. Although often referred to as just *plié*, the DEMI-PLIÉ is a knee bend with the heels firmly on the ground and is used as a PREPARATION, or push off. (The other kind of *plié* is the GRAND PLIÉ, which is almost exclusively used as

GRAND PLIÉ

a warm-up at the *barre* at the beginning of class, and consists of bending the knees, through *demi-plié*, until the heels are caused to lift off the floor with the extent of the stretch to a full squat, knees wide apart.)

Preparation is as important to execution as the step itself. Dancers prepare for leaps with little running steps and *demi-plié*, for turns with *demi-plié* and arm positions, and for lifts with some combination of running steps, *demi-plié* to push off from the ground, and the use of the arms, such as the ballerina's hands on her partner's shoulder.

PREPARATION (DEMI-PLIÉ)

In the execution of movements *en l'air*, height is not as important as the quality of SUSTAINING. Like a freeze frame in film, the danseur should project the sensation of having paused a moment at the apex of his leap. Dancers such as **Rudolf Nureyev** brought forth gasps from the audience because they were able to get so much higher than human bodies were thought capable. But the true superstar, as Nureyev is, does more than that—he or she also gives the impression of staying midair a moment before coming back to earth.

In addition to sustaining the movement to suggest the sensation of pausing in the air, leaps are judged by their landings. Quiet and stable are the key words for landings—no thuds should be heard when the dancer uses the toes and ball of the foot, again going into a *demi-plié*, or bending the knee of the supporting leg, when arriving *à terre* (on the ground) again. The feet should be steady for the landing as well. In other words, there should be no wobbly ankles, no slipping of the body or adjusting of the feet.

Both preparation, or takeoff, and landing for any jump should be quiet and steady, with a minimum of visible effort. Audiences should also be on the lookout for pointed toes whenever the feet are in the air, and straight knees, except during preparatory and landing *pliés*.

Soviet dance style tends to accentuate the pose at the end of a leap and emphasize the preparation at the beginning. But that is style, not technique—the leap must still be performed accurately. Balanchine is known for having removed the emphasis from preparation, such that sometimes there is almost none for a difficult maneuver, be it leap or turn. (There are exceptional dancers, such as **Baryshnikov**, who can actually execute very high leaps without seeming to prepare, or *plié*, at all.) While preparation is a necessity for most leaps, turns, and lifts, it should be nearly imperceptible, certainly not prominent.

Getting into the air uses a combination of momentum—from running steps, or other steps from the vocabulary that can be used for preparation, such as *assemblé*—and *plié*. If properly executed, the *demi-plié* gives the most solid base of support for the body. The dancer lets the floor help him or her by pushing off, first with the heel, then using the rest of the foot, employing especially the strength of the ball of the foot and the flexibility of the toes for that final shove. This is all done with such control that the preparation becomes simply a part of the leap. Landing is accomplished exactly in reverse, with *plié* all the more essential, since in this way much of the impact of landing is dispersed; if the leg is straight, the spine will be jarred.

The leg upon which the dancer lands, is called SUPPORTING, while the other leg is called WORKING. For instance, if the danseur lands after a leap onto the right foot with the left leg extended behind him, the right leg is called supporting and the left is called working. It may seem that the supporting leg

PASSÉ OR RETIRÉ

is doing the work, but the concept of working leg comes from that which is going to do the articulating, or make the next move. If all the dancer's weight is on the right, or supporting, leg, then it naturally follows that the next move must be made by the left. During a turn, or *pirouette*, the supporting leg is the one the dancer is pivoting upon; the working leg is the one raised off the ground in a variety of positions.

Leaps from one foot to the other are referred to collectively as **jetés**. A **grand jeté** is the most commonly seen leap. To perform a *grand jeté*, the dancer kicks the forward leg straight out in front, while simultaneously extending the back leg as he rises into the air. At the apex of the leap, both legs may stretch out a little further, so as to produce splits.

In more complicated versions of the *grand jeté*, the danseur may switch legs while in the midst of the leap; in other words, if the right leg begins the kick and is in front, when the danseur approaches the apex of the leap, he will kick his left leg forward while brushing the right leg back, to finish the splits with his legs in opposite positions.

Preparation for the *grand jeté* usually consists of a running start, or, at the least, three little running steps, before a deep *demi-plié* to push off the ground. Broken down, the leap might look like this: run left foot, run right foot, run left foot with *demi-plié*, brush forward with right foot and kick up while left foot simultaneously pushes off the ground. The right leg leads while in the air, extending into straight knees and pointed toes, while the back—or left—leg extends behind with straight knees. Then, the front leg begins curving downward to complete the leap, landing first on the right foot, in *demi-plié* of the right leg, and with the left leg extended behind.

A variation on the *grand jeté* is the **grand jeté en tournant** (or **tour jeté**), a rotating leap done by making a one-half twist in the air so that the dancer lands facing the opposite direction. For instance, if the right leg starts the *jeté* by kicking

GRAND JETÉ

---

forward, after the half turn in the air, the right leg is landed upon (the body is now facing back in the direction from which it started), and the left leg brushes through to extend out-stretched behind.

The **tour en l'air** means spinning two or three times in the air with the entire body in a vertical, legs together, toes pointed.

In the **entrechat** (braiding or interweaving), the feet exchange front to back rapidly around the ankle, with the toes pointed toward the ground (the legs resembling egg beaters). This form of *allegro* movement is named by number; for example, *entrechat quatre* means that the feet have crossed four (quatre) times in the air, though on stage it will happen so fast that the feet appear merely to be fluttering. (Note: Even the numbers in ballet terminology are in French.)

For **turns à la seconde**, the leg is extended straight out to the side, at a ninety-degree angle to the upright torso. This pose is actually an *en l'air* version of the basic second position, only one foot is on the ground and one is in the air.

ENTRECHAT

Turns *à la seconde*, are either done on *half pointe* (on the ball of the foot), like a *pirouette*, or with the supporting foot flat on the floor. Spotting must be used for these turns, just like any other, for the dancer's job is to remain in the same place on the stage for the entire number of turns. Turns *à la seconde* are somewhat the male equivalent of the female spectacle, the *fouetté* turn, in that danseurs usually perform a series of them, building speed, astonishing the audience.

TURN À LA SECONDE

Although women also do turns *à la seconde*, *grand jetés*, and *allegro* work, the ballerina is admired traditionally (as opposed to the male) for her balance (*adage*) and her extension. **Adage** comes from *adagio*, a musical term meaning slow, as opposed to *allegro*, fast or quickly. *Adage* also refers to the central part of the traditional ballet class, which focuses on placement, line, and balance.

Elements integral to **extension** are *passé* and *développé*. The **passé** (passed), is a position through which the dancer's foot must pass to get to another pose. The lifted, or working, leg is bent, toes against the knee or upper thigh of the supporting leg. The more correct *passé* has the toes high on the supporting leg, the knee of the working leg turned out far to the side. This same position, if held as a pose on its own, (as, for instance, for a *pirouette*) is known as RETIRÉ.

The **développé** (developed) is an unfolding of the working leg from *passé* into an outstretched position in the air. As the first portion of almost any *adagio* movement, *développé* is a process, not a pose, similar to *passé* being a position *through which* the leg passes, but not held as a pose in and of itself.

Finally, EXTENSION refers to raising and holding the working

DÉVELOPPÉ

leg in the air. Extension is the end result of the *développé*. The leg may be extended in front of the body, *en avant*; to the side, *à la seconde*; or behind the dancer, *en arrière*.

This last, the *développé* into an extension *en arrière*, has another name, **arabesque**. ARABESQUE describes a stationary pose standing on one leg, the back leg extended behind, knee straight, toes of the leg that is *en l'air* pointed. (If the leg is extended to the back but the toes are on the floor, that is known as *tendu* back, one of the first exercises at the barre.) A dancer can either *développé* into *arabesque* or lift the leg straight up, knees of both legs remaining straight, into *arabesque*. (*Arabesque* refers to the final, stationary, pose—not the movements required to get there.)

Arabesque may also be done PENCHÉE, or bent forward. This refers to bending the torso forward, while the extended leg correspondingly raises higher (analogous to a teeter-totter). Some *penchées* can become vertical splits, the torso bent forward until the ballerina's nose is nearly against the knee of

ARABESQUE

ARABESQUE PENCHÉE

the supporting leg, the working leg straight up in the air at ninety degrees to the floor.

Another frequently seen position of the leg in *adagio* is **attitude**. In *attitude*, the leg is outstretched behind, bent at the knee, calf and thigh on the same plane, which is parallel to the ground. (In other words, from *arabesque*, one might simply bend the outstretched leg at the knee in order to acquire an attitude, but the foot must not drop below the level of the thigh.) A variation of this is the Soviet *attitude*, in which the toes of the extended leg reach up toward the head, the calf therefore being much higher than the thigh.

ATTITUDE

Turns, or **pirouettes**, can be done in almost any pose, including the *arabesque* and *attitude* just described. The most basic *pirouette* is executed on one foot, with the working leg, or the one off the floor, in *passé*, or *retiré*. The pirouette may be done as a single, double, or triple, referring to the number of revolutions made before the dancer puts the working leg on the floor again. Turns are executed outward (*en dehors*, away from the body), or inward (*en dedans*, toward the body).

The preparation for a *pirouette* is often done with the feet in fifth, fourth, or second position, both legs in *demi-plié*. The push-off then takes place with both feet; one goes up into *retiré*, while the other—which is the foot being turned upon—elevates either into half toe or full *pointe*. This preparation helps give the dancer momentum for pivoting. The male turns with the supporting foot (or one on the ground) on *half pointe* (on the ball of the foot) while the female is *sur les pointes* (on the toes).

It's usually harder to come down and go back up again between turns than it is to sustain the momentum for a multiple turn executed while *remaining* either on *pointe* or half toe. The latter requires building momentum for turning, while the former takes more foot strength and agility. Going from flexed foot (flat on the floor) to a full *pointe* entails a number of muscle changes; going up and down on and off *pointe* while turning also requires bending and straightening the supporting knee; finally, this maneuver demands the ability to adjust balance frequently. To successfully perform this kind of turn, the dancer must keep the torso stable to ensure balance, and turn while simultaneously going up and down off *pointe*.

To get up on *pointe*, the ballerina pushes off the ground using calf and thigh muscles, forcing the arch of her foot outward by pressing first the ball of the foot into the floor, then rolling up the back of the toes until she is standing on the fleshy pads, not the actual tips. This *relevé* (raised) is why it is more difficult for a dancer to perform quick movements that raise and lower from *pointe* to flat foot than merely staying up on *pointe*. The former requires tremendous strength and agility in the foot; the latter is more a question of maintaining balance.

A second technique for gaining the altitude of her toes is the **piqué** (pricking), for which the ballerina steps—forward, back, or to the side—directly onto her toes with a straightened knee while pushing off with a small *plié* from the other leg.

FOUETTÉ

Fouettés, or whipped turns, also require the ballerina to raise and lower herself on and off *pointe*. In this type of *pirouette*, the working leg opens from *passé* to *seconde* (to the side), or to fourth position, while the supporting foot lowers off *pointe*, at the end of each revolution. The working leg then whips back into *passé* for the next turn as the dancer raises onto her *pointes* again. In other words, she holds her leg straight out to the side of her body while the supporting leg is in *plié* with the foot flat on the floor; then, bending her working leg, she "whips" it rapidly in so that the toes touch the knee of the supporting leg (*passé*), while simultaneously pushing off from the ground with the supporting foot and raising up on *pointe* again for another revolution.

Usually executed in a series, *fouetté* turns require tremendous stamina and strength in the back. *Fouettés* can also be double or triple, that is, with two or three full turns between each whipping out of the leg. Although *fouettés* are—very occasionally—specifically choreographed to be executed while traveling downstage, the normal challenge to the dancer is to stay in one spot on the stage while turning, always lowering the supporting foot to the exact same spot on the floor. Finally, after building up much momentum, *fouettés* are applauded for the dancer's ability to stop such an intricate movement with ease and total security. Without losing balance, wobbling, or shifting the feet, the ballerina should complete the turns in a stable pose.

Although *fouettés* are choreographed into many solos, thirty-two at once—such as in the Black Swan variation from Act III of *Swan Lake* or the *Don Quixote pas de deux*—have become famous over the centuries. The Black Swan set of *fouettés* is a particular challenge to a ballerina and one which has become a traditional audience favorite, such that the female solo is preceded by an air of anticipation throughout the house. (Audiences have been known to actually count the turns while she does them.) Some dancers increase the drama by doing these *fouettés* at a faster tempo than usual.

No explanation exists as to why these *fouettés* are more exciting than those in any other ballet, except perhaps because it is a well-known fact that thirty-two are required in that specific solo. And maybe there's something of a mystique to a particularly difficult dance step that every famous ballerina has been attempting since 1895 when **Pierina Legnani**, *prima ballerina assoluta*, incorporated her celebrated thirty-two *fouettés* into the coda of the Black Swan *pas de deux* of the third act of *Swan Lake* in St. Petersburg. Legnani reputedly wanted to show off her *pointe* technique. *Fouettés* certainly do that—and they've also become a means of comparing famous ballerinas over the centuries.

Other turns in the repertory are also difficult, including the *piqué*. As previously described, *piqué* refers to the way the ballerina pricks into the floor on her *pointes*. Stepping directly onto the toes of the supporting foot with a straight leg, the working leg smartly strikes a *retiré*, the turned-out knee providing some of the momentum for the turn. The preparation comes from the *demi-plié* of the working leg this time. After each revolution, the working leg comes out of *retiré* to become the leg landed upon with the knee in *plié*. Then, the supporting leg pricks out onto the toes again, knee straight all the time, for another turn.

Piqués are "traveling" turns, performed while moving across the stage, diagonally or in a circle, instead of in one place like the *fouetté*. For that, the ballerina is applauded for her ability to remain in one place. For *piqués*, she is commended for her control of the series of turns as she maintains proper direction across the stage and stops the turns in one place—which is not simple after building up that kind of momentum and speed.

Variations on this kind of turn include other poses for the working leg, such as in *attitude* (front or back), or *arabesque*. An even more difficult turn to perform is with the leg *à la seconde*, because the outstretched leg slows momentum.

In order to maintain balance while turning, either "in place" or while traveling, dancers SPOT. The head snaps around so that the eyes can stay glued on one spot in the distance. Spotting thus is a method of fixing the focus in one place to avoid getting dizzy. The head looks in one direction while the body turns, instead of keeping the neck in line with the body's movement. The neck pivots around at the last second so that the head appears to stay in place while the body turns. Spotting is crucial during all turns, but is especially useful for traveling turns, such as those in a circle, when the spot, or focus point, changes with each revolution.

Turns aren't always done just on one foot. **Chaînés**, or "chains," are a series of quick turns done in a sequence across the stage. The feet stay close together, usually in first position or shifting very quickly from first to second and back to first position again (the closer the feet, the faster the turn). If the dancer changes arm positions while traveling, the turns become more difficult because movement in the upper body can throw the dancer off balance.

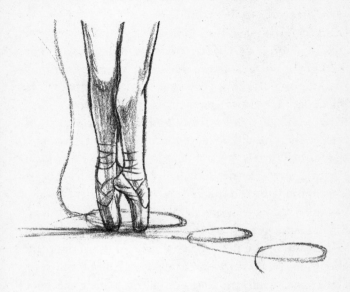

CHAÎNÉ TURNS

Momentum for a *pirouette* comes from turning out the knee of the working leg (or opening the thigh more to the side) and pushing off from the floor with the supporting foot, while the supporting leg is in *plié*. Dancers say to think *up* rather than *around*. The arms also play an important part in *pirouettes*. The preparatory *plié* is done either in fifth position with feet together, or fourth, for a wider base of support (this position is used especially for turns in which one leg is elevated, such as turns in *attitude*, *arabesque*, or *à la seconde*, when the leg is outstretched directly to the side). Arms for the preparation are usually held with one in front and one to the side.

As the turn begins, the outside arm (in second position) pulls quickly into center, thus aiding the body to pivot.

Control—keeping the upper body aligned—is what to watch for during turns. So is stopping: the ability to come out of a series of turns on *balance* is as important as speed and stability while executing them.

Baryshnikov has an uncanny ability to slow down his turns midway, change the tempo of his *pirouettes*, or come to a halt during the last turn as if stopping the speed of the revolutions were as simple as putting on the brakes. This rarity, while wonderful to see in performance, is a personal secret. After all, he'll tell you, "if there were a book of prescriptions on how to dance, there would be more than a few great dancers."

One last form of turn is the **promenade** (to walk). *Promenade* means pivoting slowly on the supporting foot while maintaining a certain pose with the rest of the body. These turns take place during very slow sections of *adage*. The dancer usually stands in a set pose, such as in *attitude*, *arabesque*, or *à la seconde*. Then, he or she pivots very slowly on the supporting foot without raising it into half toe. The ball of the foot becomes the axis, while the dancer slightly adjusts the heel for each segment, also changing eye focus for each quarter turn.

Promenade is also frequently seen in partnering work when the ballerina holds a particular pose—usually *attitude*, *arabesque*, *retiré*, or *à la seconde*—on *pointe*, one arm in the air, the hand of the other arm resting on her partner's hand or shoulder while he walks a full turn around her, pivoting her body as he walks. Sometimes the danseur also supports his partner in her pose with a hand on, or arm around, her waist. In other words, the ballerina stays in one place—pivoting on *pointe*—while her partner, who is supporting her, walks around her.

Dancers' training includes classes specifically for the technique of partnering, which includes lifts, supported turns, *adagio*, and unison dancing. All of these require timing and balance, with a hint of danger and élan.

Pas de Deux

Translated literally from the French as "step for two," **pas de deux** refers to partnering, or couple dancing. Codified in Russia in the 1860s, the **grand** or **standard** *pas de deux* formula consists of *entrée* and *adagio*, for the couple together; a solo for the danseur; a solo variation for the ballerina; and CODA, or finale.

Pas de deux allow each dancer to display specialties. In *pas de deux* of the classical tradition, the first male solo emphasizes leaps; his second, shorter solo in the coda, usually consists of turns. The ballerina may exhibit extension and balance in her first solo and flashy turns in the coda to match those of her partner.

Partnering requires an intuitive language and careful teamwork. Much of the unspoken communication that partners need in order to perform onstage together is established during rehearsals. Edward Villella once demonstrated how partners "speak" to each other onstage: they talk through their hands. Most partnering work involves holding hands—in partnered pirouettes, promenade, and *adagio* balances, such as *arabesque penchée*, the ballerina's weight is not leaning on her partner, it is simply supported as the two of them hold hands. Not a tight grip, this is a relaxed connection in which the hands are in almost constant motion, adjusting, modifying, shifting pressure to accommodate the balance, moves, weight, and needs of the other. Sensitivity to these changes makes a dancer a good partner.

The ballerina must not depend totally upon her partner for support. In most lifts, there is a preparation that helps send her body into the air—and takes the weight off her partner. This preparation may be little running steps toward him before flying up into the air, a *plié* as for a jump off the ground, or a push-off by placing her hands on his shoulders or wrists and then straightening her elbows. For *adagio* and turns, the ballerina should be able to be ON BALANCE (steady on her feet alone in any pose) without the aid of his hand.

Pas de deux appear in a variety of ways. Some are choreographed specifically to be performed in an evening that includes several short ballets, or several excerpts, such as *divertissements*, from full-length ballets. Other *pas de deux* are taken directly from ballets. For instance, the *Don Quixote* and *Le Corsaire pas de deux*, while taken from story ballets, are most often performed as show pieces on their own. Other well-known *pas de deux* occur within the framework of full-length ballets and comprise the "chestnuts" of classical ballet: from *Swan Lake*, the Act II *adagio* or the Black Swan *pas de deux* from Act III; Aurora's wedding *pas de deux* from *The Sleeping Beauty*; *Romeo and Juliet* balcony scene. These *pas de deux* are seen within the context of the ballet story when it is performed in its entirety, and are also performed separately.

Pas de deux, therefore, can be extracted as performances on their own, or choreographed as simply a dance for two. A *pas de deux* also occurs in a larger ballet whenever male and female are dancing together, employing some of the techniques mentioned above, such as supported turns and *adage* balances, and of course, lifts.

The prescribed formula of the standard, or classical, *pas de deux*, was created originally for the Russian classics, such as *The Sleeping Beauty* and *Nutcracker*. While not all contemporary choreography for the *pas de deux* follows the classical form exactly, the format is similar for most full-length ballets.

First, the couple does an *adagio* together, spiced with a variety of fancy lifts and clever balancing. After gracefully extricating themselves from whatever complicated pose completes the *adagio*, the couple bows formally and walks offstage.

Applause almost always interrupts the continuity of the *pas de deux*. However, it is entirely appropriate to applaud after each section, or variation, as well as in the middle of the dancing itself when a difficult maneuver is executed with particular finesse.

The danseur now begins a solo designed to show off his virtuosity, usually including a series of spectacular leaps diagonally across the stage. After a grand finale of circular or aerial wonders, he alights either in a standing pose or on one knee.

The ballerina's turn comes next while her partner catches his breath backstage. Her contrasting variation exhibits *pointe* work and balance at a slower tempo. Her VARIATION, or solo, concludes with high-speed turns or another traveling feat, such as hopping on the tip of one *pointe* shoe, the other leg staying ramrod in place, until she stops totally still for a bravura pose and exits to a swell of applause.

This signals the danseur to enter from the wings and spin, which he will do at top speed to commence the coda, or conclusion. He stays onstage after this solo section to watch his lady enter with a dazzling set of *pirouettes*. (*Fouettés* are likely to appear here.) After this "competition" (sometimes —and especially as performed by the Russians—these *pas de deux* look like anything-you-can-do-I-can-do-better), the couple join for a flashy set of lifts and partnered turns and one final, spectacular pose.

For contemporary *pas de deux*, or for couple dancing within the context of a ballet, these exact sections may not appear or not in this exact order. But the same techniques of good partnering—and many of the same well-known lifts and poses—will.

The art of *pas de deux* brings to mind the traditions of courtly love: the man's role is to make his partner look as beautiful and accomplished as possible. Working with someone requires a different set of skills than dancing alone. Ideally, the male should be taller than the female (and she is about two inches taller than usual in her *pointe* shoes). He must be strong enough to lift her easily, and their proportions should look appropriate when dancing in unison.

Some sections of *pas de deux* consist of the two dancers performing the same set of steps together, side by side. It's not all lifts, supported balances, and intricate togetherness.

Cynthia Gregory, longtime prima with ABT, had a difficult time finding the perfect partner due to her height (5'7"). "I can't spend time hunting," she once remarked, "so I'll just dance with everybody." (She said **Nureyev** was her favorite partner.) Many dancers give the illusion of being quite tall onstage, but are surprisingly petite in person. **Suzanne Farrell** was so statuesque onstage it seems impossible that she is only 5'6". (Likewise, **Nureyev**, **Villella**, and **Baryshnikov** are such giants in the dance world that one automatically assumes them to be taller than they are.)

Lifts demand a certain sensitivity—as well as strength. Although most danseurs work out with weights to strengthen their arms and shoulders, getting a ballerina into the air, or onto a shoulder, or tipped toward the ground, is often accomplished with the legs.

Both dancers do a preparation before the ballerina goes into the air. She may do little running steps toward him or a combination of steps designed to gain momentum. The important part is the last-minute *plié* (knee bend) from which each pushes off.

In some instances, the danseur lifts the ballerina from a static pose, such as straight up into the air from her *arabesque*, so that he must withstand her entire weight. For this lift, the danseur may support the ballerina with one hand under her thigh, the other under her rib cage. In most other lifts, however, she does her share of the work by jumping into the air simultaneously with his lifting. Coordination and timing should give the impression that she is flying into the air on her own. Some *pas de deux* choreography focuses almost all the attention on the female, the audience almost not feeling the presence of the male.

The coordination of two bodies into aerial configurations is a matter of melding the physical proportions and movement of each during rehearsal. Every dancer has a particular way of dancing that has a lot to do with body type and personal style. Partners must be aware of one another's methods of doing lifts—and they must develop a sense of the other's PLACEMENT (where the other's body is in space) in order for her to balance on him during lifts, and for him to support her during turns and *adagio*. It's one thing to practice a *pirouette* alone, hour after hour, until certain of a solo passage. It's another matter altogether to feel confidently in sync with a partner.

There's no shortcut to this, only practice. Those assured smiles you see during performance often belie the tedious hours of work necessary to conform one physical body to the needs and capacities of another. (In spite of what may appear to be either overt or intimated sexuality between couples, dancers are paying attention to the dancing—not coming on to one another. The rehearsal process depersonalizes the context.)

New partners need rehearsal time to maneuver around each other until a sense of timing and balance is achieved. Lifts in and of themselves are usually worked out in rehearsal—many of them have a specific technique—but there is always the slight difference in body size and performing style that needs to be understood. Lifts also are modified by the choreographer; when a new lift is created, danseur, ballerina, and choreographer work together in the studio to devise the method of coordinating it.

One common type of lift is the one-handed or **pole lift**, which looks as if the ballerina is sitting in the palm of her partner's hand, directly over his head.

POLE LIFT

The **fish dive** is a traditional favorite in which the ballerina is scooped up at the waist from an *arabesque* so that both legs are behind her. Her partner then balances her body on his own, with her torso bent close to the ground, her legs either resting on her partner's bent knee or tucked behind his waist. Each set of partners has a secret method for this no-hands phenomenon.

FISH DIVE

In the **shoulder lift**, the ballerina is lifted straight into the air to "sit" on the danseur's shoulder. This lift is often used for the pose at the end of a ballet, or *pas de deux*.

Lifts often include **supported jumps** for the ballerina. For instance, she may do a *grand jeté* with her partner's hands on her waist (often she puts her hands over his wrists for added push-off), so that her jump goes even higher. Or he lifts her, again by the waist, while she does *entrechat* (beats of the feet around the ankle) or splits, kicking both legs out to the side simultaneously.

Bravura lifts are often used to end a *pas de deux*. An audience favorite is the overhead *grand jeté*, in which the ballerina is lifted upside down over her partner's head. Her torso is bent back, so that her upper body and arms appear to drip down his back, while she extends one leg almost straight up in the air above her. This is an example of a frequently seen lift that requires learning one another's point of balance.

OVERHEAD GRAND JETÉ LIFT

Lifts require control, in addition to strength and timing. Bringing the ballerina back down safely is as important as getting her into the air, in the same way that the landing is as important as the takeoff in leaps. The ballerina may be brought down to land *sur les pointes*, on *demi-pointe* (or half toe), or with her feet flat on the ground. Sometimes the maneuver requires putting her down onto *pointe* and then lifting her again immediately into the air, for a light move. Other times the lift is completed with the ballerina in *demi-plié*, so that she can take off again for another supported lift (in this case, her partner usually has his hands around her waist). The danseur must also be careful to place her exactly where she is supposed to be on the stage and on balance, so that she can dance off on her own. Frequently when lifts end, the ballerina is required to dance away from her partner, so it is important that she not be thrown off-balance by him, or be leaning on him when she lands.

Turns are either supported by the danseur's hands on either side of the ballerina's waist, or are **finger turns**, which means she grasps the middle finger of her partner's hand, which is held directly over her head. When it's time to stop revolving,

FINGER TURNS

he either grabs hold of the waist he has heretofore been pushing around like a merry-go-round, or he closes the rest of his
fingers around her hand in a fist to stop her momentum.

During *adagio* sections, the danseur supports his partner in
her **développé extensions**, either with hands around her waist
or holding her hands. Her leg may be lifted in front of the
body (*en avant*); to the side (*à la seconde*); or to the back (*en
arrière*), in either *attitude* (bent knee) or *arabesque* (straight
leg stretched out behind). This is where *développé* is most likely
to appear. Getting the leg into the positions described above
requires passing the foot up the calf to the knee of the supporting leg (*passé*), then extending the foot so that the leg
opens from the knee up—and up—and up (*extension*).

When the ballerina's leg has reached the apex of the extension, the danseur may loosen his support of her hand, so
that her fingers are resting very lightly on top of his hand,
usually held in a fifth *en haut* (above the head) position of
the arms. The ballerina then finds her own balance, lets go
of his hand, and holds the position *sur les pointes* without him.
For this move, she is applauded for the length of time she can
balance on *pointe* and the fact that it is difficult to make the
transition from being supported to balancing on her own.

Other supported partnering work is also a combination of
the ballerina's being held by her partner and then let free to
balance on her own. These maneuvers require a sensitivity to
one another's balance. For instance, after letting go to balance, as described above, the ballerina may then swing her
extended leg into an **arabesque penchée** (where the torso is
bent toward the floor in exact opposition to the raising of the
leg, like a teeter-totter). Her partner, who was standing behind
her for the extension, will let her go for her balance, then
perhaps drop to one knee so that his arm or shoulder is there
for her to lean on when she completes the *penchée*. Once
again, learning the timing of the other dancer is of the essence.

SUPPORTED EXTENSION

This same type of letting go and trusting occurs in the familiar **drop** to one side: the ballerina stands with both feet in fifth position *sur les pointes*. She then lets her body lean to one side as an entire unit. Her partner shifts position from standing directly behind her to the side toward which she is leaning so that he'll be behind her torso as she completes the drop, usually catching her around the waist, or under her armpits. This maneuver requires a lot of trust on the ballerina's part, since this pose actually consists of falling into his arms.

The difference between good and great partners shows up most when watching the same ballet with different casts. A good team will make dancing together look effortless; there will be a smoothness to the complex arm and hand changes they do together during *adagio* sections. Lifts will be executed with a certain bravura, with a sense of going beyond rather than holding back. The ballerina may hurtle herself into the air for a flying lift or let go with more abandon when her partner is expected to catch her. When timing and placement matter most, theirs will be impeccable; when she finishes her solo turns, he is right there, exactly behind her to catch her for the lift which follows. Their trust is communicated to the audience, who can enjoy the performance more sensing this confidence.

Some couples have become known for working well together as a special team, such as **Rudolf Nureyev** and **Margot Fonteyn** (Royal Ballet, England), **Mikhail Baryshnikov** and **Gelsey Kirkland** (American Ballet Theatre), **Suzanne Farrell** and **Peter Martins** (New York City Ballet), **Marcia Haydée** and **Richard Cragun** (Stuttgart Ballet), and the late **Erik Bruhn** and **Carla Fracci** (formerly with American Ballet Theatre). Like Lunt and Fontanne of the theater, these are dancers that have a special chemistry beyond the physical coordination of their timing together.

During the days when they were partners, **Kirkland** said about Baryshnikov: "Dancing with him is like conversation. The physicality of dancing together is wonderful. But you can't describe how spiritual a partnership is. Feelings flow back and forth. Maybe it's because we do care about each other and I not only respond to him as a dancer but as a person." **Baryshnikov**'s version of *pas de deux* is: "I can't help but be a little in love with all of my partners."

While all professionals are capable of dancing well with any partner, some work better together than others. Finding the perfect partner is very important to dancers; often it is a trial-and-error search. Generally, the artistic director makes the decision who will dance with whom in performance. Some dancers have many partners in one company; some "guest" in other companies in order to have the opportunity to experience working with different partners. Occasionally, a particular casting yields the ideal partnership—the couple understands each other intuitively, has a feel for the other's dancing that doesn't require rehearsal explanation, or they have the right physical proportions for one another. In other words, a perfect match.

Dancers usually must perform with many different partners. True professionals know their steps so well that they are able to make slight adjustments to fit a partner's particular way of moving. Unless dancers are content doing *divertissements* (bravura solos from full-length ballets, such as the *Nutcracker*), their careers are going to revolve around partnerships. The principal parts in most ballets are designated for a couple who perform at least two *pas de deux* together in the course of an evening. Flexibility, or even compromise, can be the ambitious dancer's greatest friend, since those aforementioned gifted partnerships are a rarity.

More often, an international reputation is achieved through appearing with many different partners, sometimes in many different companies as well. So no matter how they feel about one another offstage, it behooves the professional couple to arrive at some sort of understanding while on.

Rudolf Nureyev explained the concessions partners make during rehearsal: "It's like balance. You can't just do your own thing, regardless of other people. You have to respond. It is discussion about every aspect of the role and every moment of given choreography. Two different opinions. No, *three* different opinions. There's the choreographer and there's two dancers who perceive the choreography differently perhaps. So again, it's discussion to find common ground.

"If you can't find that, you compromise. You regret the performance is not going to be memorable. So one day it works, one day it doesn't. Then there are partners who would transcend the daily routine, who forget about the day-to-day misfortunes and give a performance."

While Nureyev declined to give specific names of partners, other dancers have, like the late **Erik Bruhn**, famous for his partnership with **Carla Fracci**. Just before his retirement, Bruhn suffered shooting pains from a previous back injury, which occasionally made lifting his partner impossible. In the second act of *Giselle*, a series of successive lifts are in the choreography to give the impression that the spirit of Giselle is flying. After struggling through several rehearsals in which Bruhn's pain mounted, he and Fracci decided to change the choreography to a solo for Fracci.

While kneeling downstage during the performance waiting for Fracci's approach, Bruhn heard a crash behind him. Fracci had fallen flat on her face. Later, he asked his famous partner what had happened: "I thought I could fly by myself," replied his assured co-star. "It felt so wonderful!" "But she never again," laughed Bruhn, "tried to do alone what she needed me to partner."

This team had a comfortable rapport. But there are tales galore of couples hissing at one another during performances, swearing through gritted teeth when the audience saw only smiles. The effortless look of practiced partnering often covers annoying flaws or angry rivalries between the pair. While the utmost cooperation is required in teamwork, dance also involves the ego. A good team will make each other look great. The vain pair will be at war. And some couples just don't see eye to eye, no matter how hard they try. None of this, however, should affect their performance.

Again, **Erik Bruhn** shared his experiences with another partner, **Natalia Makarova**. "I could get very uptight and even angry with Natasha, whereas that feeling never occurred with Carla. And that's not to indicate our relationship was such that if you don't love, then hate is involved. It borders on indifference.

"It was so much above that with Carla. If there were some problem, it was solved in some other way. But I have had confrontations with Natasha that just couldn't be avoided.

That I would like to say, she certainly provoked. She would often say that I did the same. So we stood like that, sometimes. But it's been fun, too, because the day after, is just beginning again."

Sometimes an injury requires last-minute cast changes. The primary difficulty for partners who have had insufficient rehearsal time is lifts and partnered balances, since the couple may not have achieved an accurate feeling for one another's placement.

For instance, during her career as prima ballerina with New York City Ballet, **Maria Tallchief** recalled a frightening incident. Her usual partner had been replaced by a young soloist just before a performance of Balanchine's *Scotch Symphony*. The second movement required some minutely timed tossing of Tallchief by the corps men.

On this occasion, Maria and her substitute partner "had rehearsed it, but not a great deal and in fact I'm not sure we had ever rehearsed this throw in the air. So the two boys threw me with great élan and strength. And I flew through the air, landed on my partner, and knocked him flat over. I found myself staring into the footlights, with my partner on his back and my pink tulle dress all over. He couldn't get up and I couldn't get up. We had to repeat the same throw and lift to the other side in sixteen bars of music and it took us that long to get up from the floor."

Mistakes occur onstage, however, even between veterans who are used to each other. There's a well-known *pas de deux* in the ballet *La Fille Mal Gardée* that ends in the one-handed pole lift, the ballerina seated in her partner's hand above his head. For a breathtaking split second, those in the audience who know what's coming next wonder—each and every time—if it's going to work.

Then, lo and behold, the dancers always make that impossible lift look easy. The ballerina perches aloft as if her partner's hand were as secure as a throne. And he acts as if she were featherweight.

There are other nights in the theater when holding one's breath is portentous, like the time **Rudolf Nureyev** lifted Britain's Royal Ballet prima **Lesley Collier** at the Met in New York City, near the end of *Fille*, for a pole lift. Suddenly he looked confused, and down she tumbled to the audience's unison gasp. Nureyev quickly recovered—before her head hit the floor—turning the lift into a safe, if awkward, fish dive.

Together, partners moderate their differences as dancers to allow freedom to dance with abandon: she knows she can count on him; he knows exactly where she'll be and how she'll be dancing. Getting a "feel" for one another is part of the intuition of partnering that is difficult to teach, but is an important part of the rehearsal process. While there are specific classes for the technique of partnering, much of the final product is learned through the process of dancing with different partners. In rehearsal, dancers learn each other's idiosyncracies so that they can help one another pull off a good performance. Nothing must be left to chance onstage.

Getting to this point in a dancing career takes a lot of preparation. A dancer's training is a combination of education and the building of physical prowess.

Training

Dance training can begin as young as three or as late—especially for men—as fourteen. Traditionally, ballet lessons have been de rigueur for every little girl, though more and more, their brothers are attending dance school along with them. Some professional dancers have been known to start classes in college, but they are the rare exception. Most, particularly in the ballet world, start between the ages of seven and ten.

For the youngest children, dance classes might consist of learning rhythm by moving to music, with simple steps such as skipping, hopping, gliding. Learning tempo, dynamics, direction, musicality, and how to change the emphasis for each type of movement is something every dancer needs. The earlier one learns, the better.

To embark on serious training, dance instruction needs to encompass proper development of the entire body. Since the decision to begin professional training generally takes place in a child's teen years, students of junior high-school age are watched carefully to see who exhibits both natural talent and the necessary physical abilities to dance professionally.

In **beginner classes**, whether for modern or ballet, children are taught the fundamentals of dance. The basic positions are learned first, followed by simple COMBINATIONS of the elemental dance steps. The primary purpose of dance training at this stage is to learn the required posture for dance, develop the muscles of the body, and know the names of the various steps, adding to that vocabulary year by year.

In the ballet world, there are **graded systems** of dance training. In these schools, which include for example, the School of American Ballet in New York City, the Royal Academy in London, and the Russian schools based on Vaganova technique, students are auditioned and enter while young. This is so that their bodies learn dance "in the muscles" while they are still developing. At the end of every academic year, students are evaluated to determine if they are sufficiently prepared for the next class, or grade, level. This type of evaluation and promotion continues right up to preparation for the company, or auditions for performance.

In these "graded" ballet schools, classroom uniform often indicates rank. However, the regime of clothing is strict in all ballet schools, where pink tights, pink ballet slippers, and *pointe* shoes with leotards or short rehearsal skirts are generally required for women; and white tee-shirts with black tights and black or white ballet slippers are usually the uniform for men. Both sexes keep their hair pulled back off the face during class, with the girls wearing a bun, which is good practice for their performing days ahead.

In a movement form characterized by discipline, the dancers must be disciplined in dress as well. Color may vary from school to school; sometimes the beginning students wear black leotards, progressing to pink, navy blue, or white. The color of her tights may become a status symbol for the aspiring ballerina. To be promoted from black to pink tights is a moment almost as exciting as receiving one's first pair of toe shoes. As the sheerest color, pink shows best how the muscles of the leg are working and prevents dangerous errors from going unnoticed.

Probably the most significant promotion to occur in a young female dancer's life is her first invitation to wear **toe shoes**. The legendary pink satin *pointe* shoe consists of a reinforced box around the toes and a shank placed between the inner and outer sole of the shoe. The BOX is constructed of more than seven layers of fabric and glue, which are formed flat across the front of the toes of the shoe to provide a platform on which to execute maneuvers such as *pirouettes*. Ballerinas can turn much faster on their *pointes*. The clunking noise often heard when a ballerina lands after jumping or while running across the stage is the sound of the stiff box tapping the stage floor.

The SHANK, made of pliant natural material, conforms to the arch of the ballerina's foot when she is pointing her toes. The shoes are constructed perfectly flat with no differentiation between left and right. The strength of the ballerina's foot,

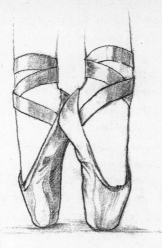

TOE SHOES

not the toe shoe, forms the lovely arch seen when she stands on *pointe*.

Pointe shoes are made entirely by hand with the result that no two pairs will turn out exactly alike. Glue and natural fibers are the only materials used. Pleats are formed in the material behind the box (underneath her toes when the dancer is standing flat), to form the basis of support. A drawstring ribbon around the top edge of the shoe holds it firmly in place, but is not sufficient to keep it safely on the dancer's foot while dancing. Therefore, pink satin ribbons are sewn on each side, then crossed over the instep and wound around the ankle. For a performance, most dancers make a knot in the ribbons, then moisten them to prevent slippage, or take a few stitches in them before cutting off the excess ribbon and tucking or sewing the ends under the knot. Some dancers also sew quarter-inch elastic at the back of the shoe that stretches completely around the ankle and keeps the heel from slipping out of the shoe. The shoe should appear smooth onstage, with no clue to the machinations that are making it stay on the dancer's foot. Only an amateur will have loose ribbons or ends showing.

Before every performance, ballerinas execute a variety of rituals to don their *pointe* shoes. Some wet the shoe's heel to help it adhere better to their tights, while others place glue inside the heel of the shoe. Preparation of a dancer's *pointe* shoes may take as long as the entire time allocated to makeup, hairstyling, and costuming.

Since all ballet shoes are meant to fit like gloves, they are purchased quite snug, so as to be almost uncomfortable. Whereas the leather of the **technique slipper** stretches and conforms to the foot fairly quickly, toe shoes must be "broken in" until shoe and foot become a unit. This process is different for every ballerina, who generally has shoes of every gradation of "broken in" ready for the specific demands of each ballet she dances. For ballets such as *Giselle*, a softer box is appropriate, when landings must be quiet, *bourrées* gentle; for other types of choreography, such as *allegro* work, a harder box— giving more support—is preferable.

All those layers of stiff materials interspersed with glue that compose the box lose their body with repeated dancing—and foot perspiration. When the box becomes too soft to perform in, the shoes are either discarded or worn in place of technique slippers for class. Most ballerinas wear a new pair of *pointe* shoes for each ballet or, at least, for every performance. After dancers have left the theater, the dressing room floor is strewn with worn-out shoes—some pairs used less than an hour. (While rehearsal clothes are the responsibility of each dancer, shoes are supplied to dancers in a professional company.)

Each ballerina has her own method of ensconcing her toes in Band-Aids, adhesive tape, or lamb's wool to prevent or protect blisters while dancing for so many hours on the tips of her toes. Although feet toughen and form calluses after years of dancing on *pointe*, blood from blisters rubbed raw against the stiff box may cake and dry in the toes of *pointe* shoes. It could seem a paradox that something so beautiful onstage can cause pain, but New York City Ballet choreographer **George Balanchine** saw no reason why offstage realism should affect an audience's enjoyment of the performance: "Women who dance have ugly feet. Their feet aren't pretty anymore, but they're professional." The man who made ballet for women, a supremacy that had been developing since the day she first stood on her toes, said: "It takes fifteen years to acquire the technique of *pointes*."

The toe shoe may be most identified with ballet, but the **heeled shoe**, which was worn when theatrical dancing began back in Louis XIV's day, made a comeback as the character shoe. This simple design—a rounded toe with a strap across the instep—is worn by women for character dances in full-length ballets such as *Swan Lake, Nutcracker,* and *The Sleeping Beauty*. CHARACTER DANCES refer to either folk dances, such as those in the third act of *Swan Lake*, or *divertissements* such as in the Kingdom of the Sweets danced for Clara's enjoyment in *Nutcracker*. Members of the *corps de ballet* may also wear character shoes when they are portraying villagers in crowd scenes, such as the first act of the ballet *Giselle*, or as royalty watching the festivities for the wedding of Aurora in *The Sleeping Beauty*.

Most major ballet and modern dance companies in America have adjacent schools in which their future members are trained from childhood, such as the graded classes mentioned previously. These schools allow a prescribed style to be ingrained until it becomes habit when dancing on the stage. Companies such as Joffrey and American Ballet Theatre (ABT) have also had SECOND COMPANIES, in which promising dancers can practice performing the main company's repertory or works choreographed specifically for them—providing opportunities for new choreographers to showcase works. This second company is a marvelous training ground for all those aspects of professional dance one cannot learn in the classroom, such as applying makeup, dealing with stage fright, working as an ensemble, adjusting to different stages, touring.

The training of the professional dancer is not the same across the board, for the simple reason that schools of dance, in this country or abroad, are so very different. Those in the graded system espouse a specific technique that is taught in every class, with advancement carefully monitored. Schools attached to performing companies have their own method for developing dancers according to their own specifications of style and body type. (Auditions for major companies are often held at local dance schools across the country, with scholarships offered to those most promising.)

How long it takes to become a professional dancer depends entirely upon how long the individual needs to master necessary technique and become fluent in the basic vocabulary. (It is not unusual for girls to join a professional ballet company while in their teens; many are dancing principal roles before their twentieth birthday.) There are as many stories about either overnight success or the long, hard road to fame as there are dancers. Some learn steps more quickly than others; some have a more "natural" dance body; some work harder or have time to take more classes. A lot has to do with parental and educational support. New York City's High School for the Performing Arts, for instance, offers a flexible schedule that allows students to train professionally while taking academic classes. Elsewhere, students must wedge dance classes into afterschool hours. Those accepted into schools in New York City from other locations must live away from home, sometimes in the apartments of senior company members or other arrangements with adult supervision. Some dancers have tutors; others finish high school by correspondence.

Once accepted at a training school for dance, the students' regimentation begins. Most dancers train in ballet technique, since it forms the basis, and gives a good grasp of, fundamentals. There are also, however, many excellent schools of modern dance that train in a specific style, such as Martha Graham's School of Contemporary Dance in New York City.

In most professional full-time dance companies, the dancers begin their day at ten or ten thirty with an hour and a half technique class, either together as a company or individually at a studio where a particular teacher serves as a dancer's coach. Rehearsals are usually scheduled in the afternoon. Union rules prevent some of the burnout that used to occur. For instance, in its early days, the Joffrey Ballet traveled around the country in a station wagon, dancers performing night after night as well as handling all aspects of the performance, including tech. Now there is a strict limit to the number of hours a dancer can be expected to rehearse each day; these hours will be different during a performing season, when the dancer must take class, rehearse, and perform all in the same day.

A SEASON refers to the span of weeks when a company is performing. For example, New York City Ballet has traditionally had both spring and winter seasons at its Lincoln Center home, as well as three weeks each summer in Saratoga, New York. American Ballet Theatre, on the other hand, may have a season in New York City and then two cross-country tours. (A tour is also technically part of a season. In other words, tour performances are part of a TOUR SEASON, as opposed to when dancers are off, commonly referred to as LAYOFF, so they can collect unemployment.)

REPERTORY refers to all the dances a ballet company is currently performing. A particular ballet is considered in repertory if it can be performed several times in a given season, or year after year. A piece in repertory may be performed by several different casts, but the sets and costumes—and choreography, of course—remain unchanged.

A piece may go out of repertory for any number of reasons, but the most likely is that new works have been added. At some point it may be revived by its original company or restaged by another dance troupe (same choreography, either borrowing sets and costumes or creating new ones of its own). Repertory is changed, season by season, at the discretion of the artistic director.

Touring is another reason that repertory can change. Most major dance companies have one or two tours per year, which may be either foreign or domestic. Touring from city to city began originally as a financial exigency: most dance companies were based in New York City, where there was and is just so much performance space and so much dance audience. Paying for a theater and filling a house required lots of competitive power—not to mention money.

Touring repertory is limited by the costs of travel and the stage specifications of the host theaters. The repertory choice will probably be smaller than in home seasons, and the scenery minimal. Touring companies settle in for a few nights of mixed repertory (three shorter ballets with minimal or no scenery required) and then a RUN (several nights in a row) of a full-length ballet, so that the sets can remain intact night after night while the casts change.

Another problem posed by touring is the toll it takes on the dancers' bodies. Traveling, especially changing time zones, can be both physically and emotionally rigorous. Usually given one travel day and one day off upon arrival in the next city, the fact that dancers must continually adjust to different theaters, different stages, and strange towns, living in hotels and on restaurant food, results in their contracting either illnesses or injuries more often than during a company's home season. Therefore, cast changes on tour may be numerous.

In addition to home seasons and touring, most dance companies also have LAYOFFS, or periods in which the dancers do not work. These are actually recovery or vacation times, but are called layoffs so that dancers can collect unemployment. In the days—not entirely over—when dancing full time did not bring in full-time salary, unemployment benefits helped.

During layoffs, dancers may vacation and rest their muscles in a warm, sunny climate. Or, they use this time to improve technique by taking classes with special coaches they may not ordinarily have time for when taking company class and rehearsing. Most dancers would agree that to go several days in a row without taking technique class or at least warming up alone is disastrous. The body takes twice the time to get back in shape after vacationing.

Another opportunity for dancers when not performing with their home company is GUESTING with other dance companies, domestic or abroad. In other words, a dancer in one ballet company takes a role in a ballet being performed by another company. Some dancers have even taken a year's leave, or sabbatical, from their home company in order to guest continuously. This not only offers them chances to dance other repertory but also gives them experience working with different partners or choreographers. **Natalia Makarova** was a principal dancer with ABT; however, she also appeared as a guest artist with London's Royal Ballet. Some dancers may take a partner with them; others dance with a member of the guest troupe.

Sometimes these guesting experiences cause dancers to switch allegiance. They might, for example, use the guesting opportunity to transfer from ballet to modern dance. Others, tired of the politics of a large company, might choose a smaller one in which they can be a leading dancer. Some feel the need to change repertory or work with different choreographers. Such, for instance, was the impetus behind **Gelsey Kirkland**'s move from New York City Ballet to American Ballet Theatre. At New York City Ballet, the choreography was almost exclusively that of **George Balanchine** or **Jerome Robbins**. American Ballet Theatre, on the other hand, performs full-length, traditional classics, dramatic ballets by **Antony Tudor** and new works by contemporary choreographers. Kirkland, of course, also left for a new partner—in this case, **Mikhail Baryshnikov**—another reason to switch.

Dancers also change companies in order to improve their rank and therefore increase performance opportunities. Determination of rank is different in every dance company, but usually the choreographer chooses the dancers he or she wants to work with and create movement on. This may be a political decision but is more likely a matter of a dancer's having a particular physical type or way of moving that fulfills the choreographer's desired creative vision.

In a company of several choreographers, the artistic director has the final say regarding casting—who will dance what role, who will be the lead in a ballet, and who will dance the first night, or one reviewed by the critics, of a run which will include several casts. Who becomes the "first cast" is often baffling to the audience—the critics certainly discuss this issue as well. Individuals in the audience may have a company favorite that may or may not coincide with the artistic director's decision.

Who rises to top rank and who does not can be equally baffling. In some companies, all dancers are of the same rank. However, even in these companies, it may be clear that some dancers have the leading roles or are the leads in the company since they may dance solos in several numbers in the same evening. These decisions are up to the administration of the company, the reasons as numerous as the people making them.

Other companies clearly delineate who is a principal, soloist, and *corps de ballet*. Within these rankings, however,
changes may occur in casting. For instance, a *corps de ballet*
member may be given a solo in a particular dance. However,
the reverse will not occur—a principal won't dance in the
corps. When a vacancy occurs in the upper ranks, an artistic
decision is made as to who will be promoted, though a soloist
may be promoted to principal rank without a vacancy occur-
ring first. The artistic director may wish to use a dancer in
principal roles for upcoming new ballets.

When a new ballet is created, the choreographer chooses
the dancers with whom he or she wishes to work. While the
choreographer is explaining the steps, other dancers may be
watching, or marking the steps, behind them. Those thus
learning by proxy become a second cast or can fill in if one
of the original dancers gets injured. (In fact, knowing the
steps of other dancers in a ballet is a terrific way to get promoted, or just noticed, by management. Dancers who learn
quickly, or can fill in quickly, are valuable.)

Filling in for an injured dancer, however, is not always
possible. If a particular dancer's role cannot be danced by
anyone else, or if no one else has yet learned it sufficiently,
or if that dancer has an inimitable quality for the role, a ballet
may be cancelled from the program when that dancer cannot
perform. Many of the ballets that **George Balanchine** choreographed on **Suzanne Farrell**, as an example, were not
taught to anyone else at the time of their creation; when she
couldn't dance, the ballet was replaced for that performance.
Now that Farrell has retired, that rich repertory—consisting
of some of Balanchine's greatest work—is being parceled out
to other principal dancers in the company, thereby preventing
what might have become a startling comment on the eva-
nescence of dance. (However, Balanchine's idea may have
been the correct one. Many of his ballets, while taking on an

interesting new character with a new dancer, receive their most penetrating interpretation—especially in the case of Farrell—only by those upon whom he created the steps originally.)

In most instances, though, the second—and even third—cast either learns while the dance is being created, or in rehearsals after the ballet is in repertory. A dancer new to the company may be taught by a senior member, who either knows the dance well or has danced it often. Brand-new dancers have many steps in many ballets to learn, often feeling overwhelmed their first season.

A dancer who works hard can definitely get ahead, but the dancer who is just plain talented, or charismatic, is the dancer who will become a star. Dancing is more than a combination of steps performed accurately. **Baryshnikov** once said, ". . . in *Giselle* the steps are very simple and not very exciting on their own. So you must display them at their best, show them off. More important, even, is what you do between the steps, what you look like, what you feel down deep."

Dancing is the nuance, the feelings that dancers give to combinations of steps, as well as what their bodies do while performing them. When you observe Baryshnikov—or your own favorite dancer—closely, you'll discover yourself responding to more than just the tricks and difficult maneuvers. The *dancing* is what moves you. All the technique in the world cannot produce a great performance. The audience's kinesthetic awareness and personal sense of beauty, grace, and ease become the judging criteria. In the final analysis, inspired dancing is what motivates you to buy a ticket and attend a performance, over and over again.

CHOREOGRAPHY

Modern dance choreographer **Merce Cunningham** once said that he got ideas for dances by watching people walk down the street. On the other hand, ballet creator **Sir Frederick Ashton** believed choreography to be divinely inspired—or God dancing through him. Whichever way they start, however, choreographers do have certain elements of their trade in common.

A choreographer is the individual who combines steps together to form a dance. If it weren't for the choreographer, dancers would be improvising, or making up the movement as they went along. Sometimes choreography is collaborative, that is, a combination of ideas presented by the choreographer and elaborated upon by the dancers. Or, choreography can be created by a group, or collective, process in which the dancers suggest movement until a synthesis is agreed upon, instead of having one authority make the final decision. But more often than not a dancer's steps and sequences are the creation of one individual.

A choreographer of classical ballet has a specific movement vocabulary to work with. Like notes of music, however, these same steps can be put together in an infinite number of combinations. The prescribed steps can also be modified, as in contemporary ballet and modern dance, or repeated in different directions or done by a variety of dancers. In other words, the same step will look different in a dance depending on what step comes before and after it; the direction or tempo in which it is executed; whether it is performed while turning or leaping; what the rest of the body is doing at the same time; and how many dancers are doing it simultaneously. In short, what makes choreography interesting—instead of repetitive and boring—is the combinations of the steps. Sometimes a choreographer comes up with a combination so unique that the step itself looks new. Or, sometimes the step is repeated so differently a little later in the dance that it comes as a surprise and adds a new look to the step itself.

How the choreographer creates these combinations and turns them into a totality that becomes a dance, and not just a combination of steps, is a process that is different for every individual. Some plan it all out ahead of time, knowing exactly which dancer will do what step when and where on the stage. **Twyla Tharp** prefers this method, although she admits it requires an ability to be able to discard her plans quickly when they aren't working or if the dancers can't perform the steps the way she visualized.

How choreographers write dance down is also different for each individual. Most choreographers use a kind of personal shorthand, abbreviating words or describing movements that aren't part of the codified vocabulary, or drawing little pictures to show stage directions. Others come into the rehearsal studio with an overall picture, which is modified by the way individual dancers move. **Balanchine** let a dance evolve by watching the different abilities of his dancers. **Lar Lubovitch** describes ideas to his company and then observes how they interpret it. Choreographers can be influenced by the way certain dancers move, later creating steps to fit their individuality.

Since steps, unlike paint on a canvas, cannot be set forever, there is also space in choreography for nuance—the little tilt of the head, the slight adjustment a certain dancer makes when moving, the bold attack with which another approaches the step, all of which may change the look of the choreography tremendously.

While some choreographers work with these alterations and make use of those individualities, others are sticklers for having the movement done in an exact way that may not change. **Jerome Robbins**, for instance, may watch rehearsals long after his piece has been in performance to make certain it is still being performed exactly in the style he originally intended.

To be exact is not as easy as it sounds, considering that personality alone can affect the way a dance looks. With the body as the instrument of artistic expression, dance perhaps more than any other art form is subject to the personal— physical type, style, and emotional expression.

Choreography can be altered unintentionally with a change in casts, or when dancers leave a company and others take over the roles. In performance, too, individuals cannot help but adjust the choreography according to their special talents or shortcomings, such as extending a balance, changing the direction of a turn, or shortchanging a step on the side that is more difficult for them.

Every dancer has one side which is favored over the other. Usually one "articulates" (doing quick movements, such as beats) better, and one balances better. For instance, turns may be better done to the right than the left; balance may be better on the left foot while the right leg extends higher, or vice versa.

When it comes to the "classics" in both ballet and modern dance, the original choreography should look the same no matter who is dancing. *Swan Lake* has been interpreted by dozens of famous ballerinas—"interpretation" has to do with style, or perhaps personality, *not* the choreography. The same holds for "classics" from modern choreographers, such as **Martha Graham** or **Merce Cunningham**. Graham's *Appalachian Spring* may be performed with different dancers, but the original choreography remains the same. Cunningham's famous *Rainforest*, with decor by Andy Warhol, was in the repertory from 1968 to 1972, and revived in 1978–79, and 1988, with new casts but essentially the same choreography.

Setting the choreography on the dancers is part of the rehearsal process. The expression SET ON means to teach the choreography to the dancers. When a new work is being created, the choreographer will show the dancers the steps and have them imitate until they get it right. This demonstration is sometimes performed by a rehearsal, or choreographer's, assistant. An alternative method is for the choreographer to explain the steps verbally and then watch as the dancers carry out his or her spoken explanations. (This would be similar to how some technique classes are taught: the teacher calls out the names of the steps and then the pupils perform the combination following the verbal command without having seen the specific steps demonstrated.)

Along with the steps, the choreographer will explain the nuance, the style, the look chosen for that dance. Sometimes these rehearsals take place without music—just learning the steps to beats counted out for the dancers. Often the music is transposed for piano and the dancers learn the steps by MEASURES; hearing how the music sounds with full orchestra comes only at rehearsals much later in the process.

The differences in rehearsal approach often have to do with how closely aligned the choreography is to the music. **Balanchine** wanted his audiences to "see the music and hear the dance," so he worked directly with the piano score while setting choreography. **Lar Lubovitch** wants his dances to be visualizations of the music. **Merce Cunningham**, on the other hand, believes that dance and music should be distinct from one another, simply being performed in the same place at the same time. His rehearsals are conducted in silence with a stopwatch checking that the dancers' timing is correct.

In large ballet companies, while the "first" cast is being taught the new choreography, the second cast is standing behind them learning also. In most companies, dancers learn what others are dancing—partly so roles can be switched, partly for the pragmatic reason that dancers need fill-in's due to injury or illness.

After the premiere performance, choreography gets passed along from generation to generation by dancers who learned it originally from the choreographer. Dancers remember the steps via "muscle memory," or in their bodies, not just their minds. In the case of the classic ballets—when there was no video or notation system at the time of the first production—the choreography was taught from dancer to dancer, as it was remembered. Hence the miniscule changes in choreography which have occurred over time.

To ensure that choreography is accurately saved, two systems of **dance notation** have been created: LABAN and BENESH. Each is a form of shorthand for movement. Symbols placed at various points along a lined staff (like music) indicate where the dancer's arms and legs are to be placed and their position relative to one another. Certificated scholars either record new choreography in written form, or reconstruct former dances for performance and the archives. For example, one of the four ballets **Nijinsky** choreographed, *The Rite of Spring*, was performed less than a dozen times. In order to re-create the choreography for performance by the Joffrey Ballet in 1987, scholar and dancer Millicent Hodson studied the rehearsal notes of Nijinsky's assistant, Marie Rambert, who had scribbled her own form of notated steps in the margins along-side the musical score.

For this reconstruction, drawings by the original set and costume designer, Nicholas Roerich, also helped co-researcher Kenneth Archer suggest not only movement but the patterns formed by the dancers on the stage as well. Ballets thus lost before the advent of standard notation or film and video are painstakingly researched by historians, who use correspondence between artists, descriptions, conductor's tempi marks, and interviews from surviving audience members and original cast dancers to re-create a sense of the choreographer's intention. This process becomes a treasure hunt.

Sometimes the choreographer doesn't care about saving a piece once it has been performed. Because they are dealing with an evanescent art form, some choreographers believe that dance is for that moment, with that particular set of dancers. For instance, **Lar Lubovitch** choreographed a poignant dance in the seventies called *Girl on Fire*. It was a duet for himself and a member of his company at that time, **Susan Weber**. His company is now twenty years old and has changed the roster of company members several times since the original performance. Lubovitch has never reset that dance on two other dancers and, by now, cannot remember the specific steps. This is of no concern to him. Even now, he only videotapes performances for his personal use.

Preserving the past was also of little concern to **George Balanchine**. Focused always on the next ballet, Balanchine made no attempt to notate or remember the past ones. This job was left to members of his company who taught the steps to new dancers. Rehearsal directors (usually called the BALLET MASTER or BALLET MISTRESS) also watch with eagle eyes to make sure changes are not taking place due to sloppy dancing or misunderstanding.

Trying to re-create *Rainforest*, of which he had kept no record, **Merce Cunningham** pieced together segments of the dance from three different films of earlier performances. His biggest problem was filling in the blanks between movements that were obscured by Warhol's set—consisting of giant floating pillows—or the camera angle.

These are only some of the reasons Laban and Benesh were created. The major difficulty inherent in these systems, however, is the fact that they are difficult to learn and they are not universally known or used. Technical in nature, they tend to fall most readily into the realm of scholarship, although they also have a significant practical use as well.

With the advent of video, choreography can be saved (although not forever: tape fades and needs to be recopied frequently). Videos are useful not only for the rehearsal process. When live performances are taped, choreographers can check that the dancers' interpretation is accurate and the steps correct. In this way, they keep artistic control over their work. Also, new dancers need not spend valuable rehearsal time—and other dancers' energy—learning roles. They can study a tape of a performance. While a dancer may still need coaching in specifics not easily seen via video, this approach decreases the chance of changes in choreography due to individual dancers' interpretations.

Changes in choreography can also occur when a dance is SET ON, or taught to, a different company. *Swan Lake* is performed by dozens of ballet companies in versions as different as their artistic directors. The choreography of **Twyla Tharp** is in the repertory of several ballet companies. **Balanchine** freely offered his ballets to other companies, sending a member of his company to teach the choreography. What may change from company to company is not the overall structure or the specific steps, but the style of the piece. Here lies the pleasure in seeing the same dance over and over again—with different casts, with different companies, even with the same dancers who look different at different performances.

While there is certainly a standard that professionals maintain at all times, dancers themselves would certainly admit to having "up" days—and some performances will be different from others, not in the steps themselves but in the quality of the movement. In other words, the choreography will not be different but the performance of it will. When watching dance, look for the nuances in quality.

Interpretation is the key here—and it is different from choreography. A certain interpretation of a role has to do with an individual ballerina's concept of how, for instance, a swan queen behaves. It's the same *arabesque*, but perhaps bolder on one, more tentative on another, seductive on a third—this has more to do with individual personality or a specific dancer's style than with technique or choreography.

Interpretation and technical ability can affect the look of the choreography because style is an integral element of choreography. Dancers are asked to put the choreographer's movement onto their own bodies. It has been said, apropos of this notion, that dancers are simply tools for the choreographer. In some cases, this may be so—the choreographer wants his or her steps, concepts, and feelings for that character, role, or even pure movement, followed to the letter.

But the dancers themselves are often the inspiration for the choreography. It is one particular ballerina's way of doing an *arabesque* that caused the choreographer to put an *arabesque* at that point in the dance. So it may be impossible to differentiate who did what to whom, when it comes to choreographing. After all, the dancer is who the audience sees—not the choreographer.

Differentiating choreography from execution can be tricky when it comes to assigning quality to a performance. This ability comes with an experienced eye, but a few suggestions may be helpful: if the dancers look technically good but the dancing appears to be awkward, then it is probably the choreography which is at fault. In other words, the dancers are capable of looking better; they've been given inappropriate movement to do. If the stage patterns, individual movements, lifts, and ensemble formations are interesting but the dance appears lifeless, dull, or boring, it may be the dancers are at fault for not executing the choreography well enough to show it to best advantage. And then there's *Twyla Tharp*'s adage: "If it doesn't work, it doesn't matter whose fault it is. Bad dancing is dancing that makes people think they don't understand and they think is above them and they think they've got to be educated to appreciate. That's bad dancing."

There are instances where the influence of one particular dancer is part of the choreographic process. Some choreographers have, in fact, been linked with specific muses during their careers: **George Balanchine/Suzanne Farrell**; **Sir Frederick Ashton/Margot Fonteyn**; **Merce Cunningham/Carolyn Brown**; **Antony Tudor/Nora Kaye**. These dancers specifically suggested movements or ways of moving, which the choreographer incorporated into his vision of the dance. Although many feel that a dance so created will be indelibly stamped by the original dancer, most successful choreography will look equally good on other bodies. And while a choreographer may have at first been inspired by the physical capabilities or look of a particular dancer, the movements and themes thus created are more often than not universal. Occasionally a work will be completely lost or dropped from the repertory when a particular dancer leaves a company. Many choreographers, however, choose dancers for their companies who have a similar look and body type to previous dancers. This is probably because they like that kind of body but it also provides a certain continuity of look and serves to preserve the choreography.

In addition, many choreographers create movement "on" their own bodies; they use the movement that feels right for their own physical abilities or those steps that they themselves execute well. **Paul Taylor**, for instance, always choreographed the principal male role for himself to dance. Now that he's no longer dancing, the lead male dancer is usually of the same physical proportions and has similar dance capabilities to Taylor. To whit, he's still choreographing the way he moves.

For that matter, it's probably hard for any choreographer not to. After all, most of them were at one time professional dancers. Many demonstrate the steps themselves, although some choreographers choose to describe the movement as the dancers do it. **Balanchine**, quite a facile dancer, sometimes watched what his dancers did with a movement, then worked with them physically, twisting and turning their bodies almost as a sculptor would clay, until they arrived at the look he wanted—or, one even better.

He once said to **Suzanne Farrell**, "Can you do this?" Balanchine wasn't referring so much to specific technique as newly attempted ability; he meant doing that particular movement in that way within that combination of other steps. Sometimes what Farrell was capable of—or became capable of through experimenting—dictated choreographic possibilities.

Besides individual dancers or dance styles, choreographers are also inspired by themes, stories, quotes, poems, emotions, experiences—in addition to picking favorite music or "commissioning" music by a favorite composer. If the piece is commissioned, that means it is composed especially for that dance. The choreographer may tell the composer what idea or theme or structure or time boundaries he or she has in mind. Or he or she may simply choreograph to the new music after it is finished.

Other possibilities for the creation of a new dance include *residencies*, created by grant-giving organizations to allow dance companies space in which to rehearse and create new work while also bringing these professional companies to specific locations for longer periods of exposure. During a residency on a college campus for instance, a modern dance company's members may take turns giving technique classes to college dance students; the artistic director may give a symposium on choreography or sit on a panel with other creative artists discussing their working process; a public "master" class by the choreographer or a senior member of the company may be taught to advanced students in that particular modern technique; and—finally—the week culminates in a performance. Now one week is hardly enough time to create a new dance, but over the course of several residencies, a company might have the concentrated time and rehearsal space in which to choreograph a new work. Or, the residency may give them uninterrupted time in which to complete and polish the piece. If so, the new dance is ready to be *mounted*.

MOUNTING refers to getting the dance onto the stage for a performance. This would include set design and EXECUTION (stage parlance for painting and construction), costumes, lighting, and adjusting studio choreography to a particular stage size. This latter explains some of the need for long technical rehearsals when companies are touring their regular repertory—dances, positions of dancers, and steps may need to be altered to allow a piece to fit onto a certain stage.

Marking is sometimes used in long technical rehearsals so

that the dancers can save their energy for the run-through or the performance. To MARK dance steps means either to illustrate with one's hands or to WALK THROUGH the steps; marking suggests the movements without the dancer actually doing them. FULL OUT means dancing at performance peak—not holding back. Marking is just the opposite.

This kind of walk-through is useful both for the choreographer, who is indicating to the dancers what he or she wants them to do, and to the dancers, who would be exhausted at the end of learning choreography if they danced fully each step every moment. (One place marking won't be seen is in class, since dancers are concentrating on technique and want every step executed completely; the obvious other is during performance, where dancing takes over.)

The preparation for performance involves many different aspects besides the choreography. If the piece is a premiere, the choreographer will be consulting the costume and set designer as well. The composer will also be involved if the dance uses commissioned music. These artists work together as a team, each attempting to have an equal voice in the final look of the piece. Usually the choreographer has the final word, but every situation is different.

In the case of **Diaghilev**'s Ballets Russes and all the famous collaborations between artists (Matisse, Alexandre Benois, Bakst, Picasso, Georges Rouault, Giorgio de Chirico, Nicholas Roerich, Miró, Braque, Natalia Goncharova), composers (Stravinsky, Prokofiev, Ravel, Debussy, Satie, Poulenc), and choreographers (**Nijinsky, Fokine, Balanchine**), the impresario Diaghilev appeared to be the final voice. There have been collaborations since, such as **Balanchine** and Stravinsky, **Martha Graham** and Aaron Copland, **Merce Cunningham** and John Cage, though not on the same scale. Each contributor uses his or her expertise to make set, costumes, music,

dancers, and the dancing come together into a cohesive—
and hopefully spectacular—whole.

Dancers sometimes stop performing in order to choreograph.
Creating a role in a dance, as a dancer, is also creative, but
the parameters of the movement are set by someone else.
Working with great choreographers during their dancing careers puts dancers in touch with a variety of ways to create
movement. Dancers who become choreographers suggest that
creating movement is a natural outgrowth of a career spent
performing steps created by others. Choreography is not,
therefore, simply an outlet for the retired dancer. It results
from the yen to create one's own movement in lieu of performing someone else's. As such, it can be the culmination
of a dancer's performing experience.

Another career that often follows that of performing is one
essential for the choreographer—that of coach. Dancers who
worked closely with the choreographer for a particular piece are
invaluable when it comes to coaching those same roles. Coaches
don't teach the choreography; they preserve the choreographer's
intention. A sensitive coach acts as the interpreter for the choreographer, making certain the style, nuance, and details are
correct. **Kurt Jooss**'s ballet *The Green Table* is set on companies
by the choreographer's daughter, Anna Markard. She is most
likely to preserve the continuity and exactitude of his vision.
Former American Ballet Theatre star **Sallie Wilson**, on the other
hand, coaches roles, primarily those of choreographer **Antony
Tudor**. Wilson not only sets his ballets on various companies;
she also helps young dancers new to his choreography understand
their roles as well as the steps.

Coaches also help dancers interpret the concept of the
movement their first time in a role. This is especially important
in dramatic or story ballets, where the movement is connected
to a role, or integral to a dramatic persona.

In the same way that dances are now often referred to as ballets, whether choreographed for a classical ballet company or a modern dance troupe, this same term has become synonymous with what a choreographer creates as well. The word BALLET is used in this way to refer to the dance itself, including the choreography, music, set, etcetera. So, what a choreographer creates is a ballet—which is the same as saying a piece or a dance or a production. Calling the final product of a choreographer's work a "ballet" does not suggest that the dancing is done only in tutus and toe shoes; **Martha Graham** calls all her choreographic pieces ballets.

In the same way, choreographers today are closing the gap between ballet and modern dance. Many choreographers are working in both milieus and their works are performed by both modern and ballet companies. **Lar Lubovitch** has his own modern dance company; but his *Rhapsody in Blue* was commissioned by New York City Ballet. And **Twyla Tharp**, who began her choreography as a rebellion against—or an amalgam of—both ballet and classical modern dance, surprised the dance world when she became "artistic associate" of American Ballet Theatre (1989).

Choreographers every ballet-goer should know include **August Bournonville** (1805–1879), **Michel Fokine** (1880–1942), **Léonide Massine** (1895–1979), **Bronislava Nijinska** (1891–1972), sister of Vaslav Nijinsky, **Marius Petipa** (1818–1910)—from the annals of history; and **Sir Frederick Ashton**, **George Balanchine**, **John Cranko**, **Antony Tudor**, more recently; with **Gerald Arpino**, **Sir Kenneth MacMillan**, **Jerome Robbins**, and **Twyla Tharp** working currently. Other choreographers whose work you may encounter include **Maurice Béjart**, **Agnes de Mille**, **Eliot Feld**, **William Forsythe**, **Jiri Kylian**, **Eugene Loring**, **Dennis Nahat**, **John Neumeier**, **Ruth Page**, and **Glen Tetley**.

Each of these choreographers arrived at a specific vision

uniquely his or her own. They also created a repertory of works accessible to many audiences; their dances have been either set on several regional as well as touring companies or are likely to be performed for years. In this way, contemporary choreographers create works that may become as much classics as *Nutcracker* or *Swan Lake*. The first lastingly successful production of *Swan Lake* was, in fact, choreographed in 1895 by not one, but two choreographers. As the ballet has been handed down over the generations, Acts I and III, the scenes with court and folk dances, were choreographed by **Petipa**; the WHITE or swan acts, II and IV, were choreographed by **Lev Ivanov**, who went on to choreograph the other classic, *Nutcracker*, when Petipa fell ill. The latter's influence on ballet is exemplified by over fifty ballets he choreographed, among them most of those referred to as "classics" today: *Don Quixote*, *The Sleeping Beauty*, *Swan Lake*, *Raymonda*, *La Bayadère*. Petipa combined the softer French *adagio* style (introduced via Parisian ballet masters) with the more brilliant attack of Italian *allegro* (infused by the predominance of Italian ballerinas) to create what became a definitive Russian style.

Choreography in these classics was dictated to a great extent by historical context. As discussed, choreographers such as Petipa (called "ballet masters"—also responsible for teaching technique), were hired by the large theaters to produce their lavish spectacles. Petipa created the four-act ballet wherein the dramatic action was frequently interrupted to show off the exceptional "*pas*" of the dancers. These story ballets, in the latter half of the 1800s, incorporated his formula for inserting traditional folk dances and *divertissements*, consisting of solos and *pas de deux*—whose form was first codified in these full-length ballets. (Hence the familiar dance selections from *The Sleeping Beauty*, *Swan Lake*, *Nutcracker*.)

Choreography was often created as a showcase for technical feats due to the arrival in 1880 of the superior Italian ballerinas—such as Zucchi and Legnani—who took leading roles in most Russian productions. The long "romantic" skirt was shortened to a "classical" tutu to better display ballerinas' intricate, fast legwork and high extensions. Some dance steps frequently seen today—such as *fouettés*—were developed during this time.

From this tradition came the tendency, which survives today, for Russian choreography to specialize in what is dazzling, subordinating dramatic or emotional content to line and form. The Bolshoi, Kirov, and other troupes from the various state theaters (each one has its own ballet company) often look as if the dancers are going for the tricks. Making the technical display more important than the emotional component of the dancing is fairly typical of the Russians. Therefore, it is difficult today to determine if it is the choreography or the dancer that makes Russian ballet often appear to be soul-less. On the whole, Russian dancers concentrate on technical perfection, but the movement is often bland, as if the heart is missing. (Naturally, there are exceptions, as Maya Plisetskaya's "Dying Swan" solo, which can elicit tears when her seemingly boneless arms undulate like bird's wings, or Galina Ulanova's portrayal of Juliet; performances by these retired prima ballerinas are available on commercial videotape.)

Most of the classics, or ballets which have become part of every company's repertory and have not changed greatly over time, come from Russia. These are: *Swan Lake*, *The Sleeping Beauty*, *Nutcracker*, *La Bayadère*, *Don Quixote*, *Paquita*, and *Les Sylphides*. (Other well-known classics, which first premiered at the Paris Opera, include *Giselle*, *Coppélia*, and *La Sylphide*.)

New productions of these "standards" do occur, nonetheless. Frequently they are restaged by Russian defectors, such as **Rudolph Nureyev, Mikhail Baryshnikov, Natalia Makarova**, with their own personal changes. The version of *Nutcracker* that is aired on television every Christmas was rechoreographed by Baryshnikov. His Clara has a large dancing role, unlike the standard *Nutcracker* in which the Sugar Plum Fairy is the leading dancer while Clara is portrayed by a child. (Baryshnikov also created new productions of *Cinderella* and *Swan Lake* for American Ballet Theatre.)

It seems as if every great dancer who becomes an artistic director wants to try his or her hand—if not at choreography per se—at restaging a classic. RESTAGING refers to making a new production: it can include some new choreography, a new focus to the story, sometimes changes in use of the traditional music, sometimes new or altered roles for the dancers, and certainly new costumes and sets. **Helgi Tomasson** restaged *Swan Lake* for the San Francisco Ballet in 1987. Tomasson was formerly a principal dancer with New York City Ballet. His new vision as artistic director gave him the freedom to stage a production of the ballet that not only altered but added some choreography.

To confuse this discussion a bit further, even the Russians have restaged *Swan Lake*. The Bolshoi Ballet televised its version, with Gene Kelly narrating, with a whole new look to the "standard" choreography. Each company who thus redoes a classic puts its own stamp on it.

This is one way to tell what the signature of a company is. For instance, Tomasson's *Swan Lake* has a contemporary, young look to it, like the dancers in his company. The Bolshoi version, on the other hand, is heavy-handed and almost melodramatic: bold and brash, like what we've come to expect from the Russians. The

Kirov *Swan Lake*, on the other hand, is characterized by a purity and exactitude, almost delicate by comparison with the Bolshoi. The differences in the Bolshoi and the Kirov suggest, too, that generalities about choreography from a certain nation will hold true only so far.

In the United States, almost every town's resident ballet company stages *Nutcracker* at Christmastime. These productions may have little in common except for the Tchaikovsky music and the principal characters. Quite often the choreography is drastically altered to fit the capabilities of the dancers, or to create more roles for student performers.

Other frequently seen Russian classics are **Michel Fokine's** *Les Sylphides* (called *Chopiniana* when danced by Russian companies) and *The Dying Swan*. The former is his homage to the Romantic era, a plotless ballet performed in long white tutus. The latter is a solo to the Saint-Saëns cello music originally choreographed for **Anna Pavlova**, and also interpreted later to great acclaim by the Russian ballerinas **Galina Ulanova** and **Maya Plisetskaya**.

Fokine is primarily known for his modern reforms to ballet—requiring new styles of movement to match each ballet's theme and insisting that choreography be on a par with decor and music—which he put into practice as choreographer for Diaghilev's Ballets Russes (1909–12 and 1914), with such ballets as *Firebird*, *Le Spectre de la Rose*, and *Petrouchka*. (The latter two, originally choreographed for the legendary dancer Nijinsky, were revived by the Joffrey Ballet; their productions with Nureyev in the leading roles were televised and are available on videotape).

Not as frequently seen are the ballets of Fokine's Russian contemporaries, **Léonide Massine** and **Bronislava Nijinska**. These choreographers, along with dancer **Vaslav Nijinsky** (whose only remaining choreography is *Le Sacre du Printemps* [*The Rite of Spring*] and *L'Ápres-midi d'un Faune* [*Afternoon of a Faun*]—both performed by the Joffrey) and **George Balanchine** (who could easily be credited with creating "American" ballet), were encouraged by impresario **Serge Diaghilev**, whose Ballets Russes brought dancers and choreographers out of Russia to work with composers and artists in a collaboration considered to have given birth to "modern" ballet.

Diaghilev's chief choreographer following Fokine, during the years 1915–20 and 1925–28 was **Léonide Massine**. His ballets *Parade* and *La Boutique Fantasque*, choreographed during his years with Diaghilev, have been revived. Later, he choreographed in New York (doing a revival of *Sacre* with Martha Graham); in Europe with his own company; with Ballet Theatre; as well as with the Ballet Russe de Monte Carlo for which his *Gaîté Parisienne* (revived by American Ballet Theatre) is best known. Outstanding as a character dancer—he often danced the leading role in his choreography—Massine is also famous for creating the role of the shoemaker in the film *The Red Shoes*.

While perhaps eclipsed historically by her brother **Vaslav Nijinsky** and her many celebrated male contemporaries, **Bronislava Nijinska** was one of the formative choreographers of the twentieth century, as exemplified in the Royal and Oakland ballets' revivals (as staged by her daughter Irina) of her ballets *Les Biches* (a social satire), *Le Train Bleu* (athletic gymnastics) and *Les Noces* (Russian wedding ritual). As the only female resident choreographer for Diaghilev, Nijinska created what was hailed as the first "abstract" ballet: *Les Noces* (1923), in its architectural formations of groups of dancers, looks surprisingly similar to Denishawn modern dance.

In addition to these Russian choreographers, the works of **August Bournonville** (1805–1879) are likely to be seen in the repertory of touring ballet companies. The Danish choreographer's best-known ballet, *La Sylphide*, is often confused, because of the title, with Fokine's *Les Sylphides*. *La Sylphide* is a story ballet about a sylph (the *sylphide* of the title), who entices the bridegroom James away from his wedding with the illusion of perfect, yet unattainable, love. In this ballet and selections from *Napoli* or *Flower Festival at Genzano*, which are the primary Bournonville works seen outside the Royal Danish Ballet, are illustrated such characteristics as low, repeated leaps; the forward *jeté* with the back leg in *attitude*; lower and more rounded arms than usual; the tendency for movement to come forward toward the audience; a bounciness and lightness to the feet; and a generally cheerful countenance to the style.

In England, **Sir Frederick Ashton** (1904–1988) became synonymous with the Royal Ballet. Ashton studied with Léonide Massine and Marie Rambert (who was considered one of the two most important founders of British ballet, along with the Royal Ballet's Ninette de Valois) before becoming choreographer for the Vic-Wells Ballet in 1935—which became the Sadler's Wells and finally the Royal Ballet—where he served as associate director in 1952 and director from 1963 to 1970. Ashton has also choreographed for several other ballet companies of distinction, among them New York City Ballet and the Royal Danish Ballet, his most familiar choreography being dramatic, full-length ballets such as *A Month in the Country*, *La Fille Mal Gardée*, *The Dream*, *Enigma Variations*, and also pure lyrical ballets such as *Monotones*, or *Birthday Offering*. Ashton is also known for his remarkable collaborations with Britain's most famous ballerina, **Margot Fonteyn**, and Canadian **Lynn Seymour**.

Hallmarks of Ashton choreography include a fresh approach to the stage picture, an equal facility in both story and plotless ballets, and a sense of order and dignity that may be partially the cause of British ballet's association with purity of movement and cleanness of line. His characteristic style is shaped by soft, fluid, lyrical, and musical classicism.

Principal choreographer of the Royal Ballet since 1965, and its director from 1970 to 1977, **Sir Kenneth MacMillan** (b. 1929) uses movement to express passions, so that although his vehicle is the classic vocabulary, it becomes an articulate voice for feelings and concerns beneath the movement itself. He is best known for such ballets as *Romeo and Juliet*, *Mayerling*, *Manon*, *Elite Syncopations* (Scott Joplin, composer), *The Four Seasons*, and *Anastasia*. Many of his ballets have been staged by other companies; he was Artistic Associate of ABT from 1984–1989. Characteristic of MacMillan choreography is emotional depth in movement themes by which each character can be recognized. His partnering is unusual and varied. MacMillan creates ways for men and women to lift, fall, and spin together that are within the classic vocabulary but look brand new to the eye.

Ballet in America, on the other hand, was shaped primarily by the genius of one individual—**George Balanchine** (1904–1983). Arguably the most influential choreographer this country has known, Balanchine was pivotal in creating a look, a style, a technique, and a choreography uniquely American. While Balanchine was trained at the Russian Imperial Ballet Academy, and performed and choreographed with Diaghilev, his work for New York City Ballet was an extension of the classical technique.

Any ballet-goer will be exposed to the choreography of Balanchine, since many choreographers, teachers, and dancers were influenced by him, and his ballets appear in the repertory of dance companies everywhere. Balanchine felt no great need to preserve his choreography intact—the steps in *Apollo* were changed to reflect his vision of Edward Villella as an *en l'air* dancer as opposed to *à terre* Lew Christensen on whom he originally set it; *Four Temperaments*, now seen in practice clothes, was first mounted with elaborate costumes; in 1981, he created on Suzanne Farrell a completely new *Mozartiana* from his 1933 version. Yet, he often sent his dancers to companies the world over to stage his ballets. Additionally, several American companies have a Balanchine "look" to them, either because their dancers were trained in that style or because the companies were, or are, run by former Balanchine principals: Chicago (**Daniel Duell**), Seattle (**Francia Russell** and **Kent Stowell**), Los Angeles (**John Clifford**), Miami (**Edward Villella**), Philadelphia (**Christopher d'Amboise**), San Francisco (**Helgi Tomasson**). American Ballet Theatre and Dance Theatre of Harlem also have many Balanchine ballets in their repertory.

Balanchine created not only a new style of choreography but also a new way of moving. He felt that American energy was faster and, therefore, he wanted to increase the speed with which dancers could dance. He did this by modifying Russian technique—for instance, focusing on the toes rather than the heels during *allegro* work, thus permitting the foot to be ready to go up into the air again. Without an emphasis on floor contact, takeoff and landing are quicker; the toes do most of the work, which is more appropriate anatomically because the toes are more facile than the heel.

Due to the demands of his choreography, Balanchine, in his classes at the school he founded before establishing a dance company, unconsciously created a technique. Speed and quickness were paramount. A high leg extension was included, for both men and women. To dance his choreography best, Balanchine preferred a long and lean body type with a short torso, which accentuated the limbs. A "Balanchine" dancer, whether dancing in his company or not, will have a technical facility and ease with quick tempos, exhibit little preparation before a difficult move, execute immediate directional changes and fast footwork.

Since music was a primary motive to Balanchine's creativity (he took piano lessons and his father was a composer), musicality was tremendously important in his dancers. Balanchine shifted the emphasis in dancing from down to *up*, so that his dancers go up on the count of one (instead of up on the preparation and down on the count of one). There is, therefore, a light feeling to his ballets, as if the dancers never touch the floor.

His choreography was also greatly influenced by the different "muses" with whom he was associated over the years, a few of whom were: **Alexandra Danilova**, **Suzanne Farrell**, **Tamara Geva**, **Tanaquil LeClercq**, **Maria Tallchief**, **Tamara Toumanova**, and **Vera Zorina**. He used the particular talents of these ballerinas to devise movement; occasionally he choreographed purposely to their weak points in order to challenge them as dancers as well.

The most repeated quote from Balanchine is that "Ballet is Woman." Balanchine focused his ballets on the leading women and often created an entire career for some young dancer whom he trained and for whom he created roles befitting her personality. Balanchine altered the Russian concept of a *corps de ballet* dancing exactly in line, every arm and leg in the same position. Instead, he maintained that women dancers are like flowers: "You don't expect any two flowers in your garden to look exactly alike, do you?" His *corps de ballet* are very much individuals and although they dance together, they are not regimented, and each is expressive on her own.

Opportunities to see his work abound, even though New York City Ballet tours infrequently, and then usually abroad. Those ballets seen most often include: *Theme and Variations*, performed by American Ballet Theatre (which has staged over twenty Balanchine ballets) and the Kirov; *Serenade*, danced by the San Francisco, Cleveland/San Jose, and Pennsylvania Ballets; *Bugaku*, in the repertory of Dance Theatre of Harlem;

and *The Four Temperaments* and *Symphony in* C, by the San Francisco Ballet and Pacific Northwest Ballet; *Tchaikovsky Pas de Deux*, performed by many famous couples at galas and seen in *The Turning Point*; in addition to countless televised programs about him and his work, and the commercially available videotape of one of his last masterpieces, the 1980 *Davidsbündlertänze*.

Characteristics of a Balanchine plotless ballet (he professed that dance steps don't "mean" anything except what the viewer puts on them) would be: choreographic concentration on the music; speed and lightness; intricacy of steps in a very short amount of time, or DENSITY; high leg extensions; repetition (fairly typical in ballet—that is, whatever combination of steps is done to the right will later be done to the left); and a hierarchy to the dancing—that is, a separation of *corps de ballets*, demi-soloists, soloists, and principals. These ranks may be designated by: costume, the more elaborate for the more important dancers; placement on the stage, the more important progressively nearer the front and center; and by the order in which they dance, with the principals doing their variation last.

In these aspects, Balanchine retains the traditions of his Russian ballet background in which the hierarchy of the stage picture was: *corps de ballet* framing the stage, behind and on the sides; soloists in a different color and slighty more elaborate costume, usually on either side of center stage; principal couple, with the lady in the grandest tutu of all and usually a tiara, center stage.

After dancing with and then choreographing for Diaghilev's Ballets Russes (his best creations from that time being *Apollo* and *The Prodigal Son*), Balanchine was brought to America by Lincoln Kirstein, who financed what became New York City

Ballet. Since 1964, the New York State Theatre in Lincoln Center has been its home, built according to Balanchine's own specifications. The School of American Ballet (often referred to simply as SAB), has trained professional dancers since 1934, many on scholarship from nationwide auditions.

Balanchine's associate for many years at the New York City Ballet was **Jerome Robbins**. Like Mr. B (as his colleagues lovingly referred to him), Robbins also choreographed for the Broadway stage. (Balanchine choreographed *On Your Toes*; Robbins is most famous for *West Side Story*.) Undoubtedly because of this background as a director and musical choreographer (*On the Town*, *Peter Pan*, *The King and I*, *Gypsy*, *Funny Girl*, *Fiddler on the Roof*), Robbins melds academic and modern dance, jazz, show, and even social dance.

As a choreographer, therefore, Robbins blurs the distinction between ballet and modern, achieving a contemporary movement that doesn't always look like ballet. In his *Glass Pieces*, set to music by composer Philip Glass, Robbins's dancers spend part of the first section just walking across the stage, as if they were simply strolling down the street. (This unstudied way of moving is not generally easy for highly trained dancers.) His *N.Y. Export, Opus Jazz*, in the repertory of the Joffrey Ballet, employs the jazz idiom in a ballet context. On the flip side, Robbins choreographed pieces of lyric movement to piano, *In the Night*, *Dances at a Gathering*, and *Other Dances* which are very balletic, very lyrical. This last *pas de deux* was created for **Mikhail Baryshnikov** and **Natalia Makarova**.

Since Balanchine's death in 1983, New York City Ballet has been run by **Peter Martins** (b. 1946), a Danish-trained dancer who used to be a principal in the company, and an extraordinary partner for **Suzanne Farrell**. Martins began choreographing when he was company ballet master; now the troupe is mixing his choreography with Balanchine's, Robbins's, and an occasional contemporary choreographer commissioned by Martins as NYCB irons out its transition to a post-Balanchine dance company.

Antony Tudor (1908–1987), although British, is also included in the American choreographers' contingent because he was so influential at American Ballet Theatre where he was staff choreographer from 1940 to 1950 and associate director beginning in 1974. Tudor also worked at New York City Ballet and the Met Opera Ballet after his arrival in America in 1940. He initiated the PSYCHOLOGICAL BALLET, in which the emotions of dramatic characters are suggested through the movement. Along these lines are *Jardin aux Lilas* (*Lilac Garden*), where two lovers meet tragically for the last time at the betrothal party of one to a different person; and *Pillar of Fire*, about a young girl's initiation first into physical desire and then into the experience of love without rejection; and *Dim Lustre*, in which the action freezes from time to time as a character, suddenly reminded of a past event, is swept back in time to relive that moment.

But Tudor also choreographed humorous ballets, such as *Offenbach in the Underworld* (in the repertory of Joffrey Ballet), and *Gala Performance*, in which three rival ballerinas strive to outdo one another (performed by ABT). *The Leaves are Fading*, created on **Gelsey Kirkland** for ABT, appears to be plotless, yet there is a poignancy in the movement, as the dancers express various aspects of falling in love, that is suggestive of the decay which harbingers winter, both in nature and the human soul.

Another noted choreographer often associated with ABT is **Agnes de Mille** (b. 1909), who choreographed *Fall River Legend* and *Rodeo*. The first is the dramatic story of Lizzie Borden, accused of ax-murdering her father and stepmother; the second portrays the wild West theme of tomboy-become-lady. Although considered "ballets," the choreography evidences the influence of her Broadway work, such as *Okla-*

homa!, *Brigadoon*, and *Carousel*. De Mille modified the classic idiom, freeing the body to express emotions with a real Americana angle.

The principal choreographer of the Joffrey Ballet is **Gerald Arpino** (b. 1928), who cofounded the company with **Robert Joffrey** (1930–1988), and became Artistic Director upon Joffrey's death. Arpino's prolific repertory includes two works that became signature pieces for the company: *Trinity* and *Light Rain*. Arpino's choreography has developed through several styles over the years, each variation influenced by whatever served as the inspiration for the ballet. There were the "Berkeley ballets"—*Trinity*, a sixties peace dance to rock music; *Kettentanz*, to "lost" waltz music from Vienna found in a Berkeley music shop; *Sacred Grove on Mt. Tamalpais*, the rite of spring as set in Marin County. All of these were created while the company was in residence at Berkeley during the 1960s. Sometimes Arpino is influenced by a work of art, *Round of Angels*; a piece of music, *Light Rain*; or a concept (nuclear holocaust), *Clowns*.

While Arpino has choreographed ballets with plots and elaborate costumes, his characteristic tendency is for light material, especially unitards (a one-piece bodysuit combining leotards and tights), on lithe bodies with occasional gossamer skirts on the women, the men often bare chested. In this way, his choreography maintains the focus of dance—the human body. His dances are eloquent, usually cheerful, very lyrical and very balletic (long leg extensions for the women; fancy leaps and turns by the men). However, he creates a contemporary medium by the way he mixes movement. His pieces tend to open with dancers rushing across the softly lit stage in leaps and bounds; an *adagio* middle section with one couple—or a few—in sinuous, slinky partnering; and a finale which brings the lights on full for a big ensemble section of fast-moving, upbeat turns and leaps, including several quick, flashy solos highlighting each dancer's best qualities. In this company, dancers tend to be small, young, athletic.

In the Joffrey Ballet is also a humorous story ballet, *The Taming of the Shrew*, by choreographer **John Cranko** (1927–1973), who made his mark on the ballet world as director of the Stuttgart Ballet in Germany from 1961. He is known primarily for his full-length dramatic ballets (*Romeo and Juliet*, *Onegin*), which combine wit, technical prowess, and a use of the ballet vocabulary to create humor and tell a story. Cranko was greatly influenced by the dancers in his company with whom he worked the most, including the famous ballet partnership of **Marcia Haydée** and **Richard Cragun**.

Just when and where ballets by these different choreographers can be seen varies season to season. Repertory in major ballet companies changes constantly. In various seasons, the Joffrey Ballet may concentrate on revivals such as **Massine's** *Parade* or *The Three-Cornered Hat*, or **Fokine's** *Petrouchka*; reconstructions such as **Nijinsky's** *Sacre du Printemps* or **Balanchine's** *Cotillon*; or restagings such as **Ashton's** *Les Patineurs*, *La Fille Mal Gardée*, *The Dream*, *A Wedding Bouquet*. American Ballet Theatre tends to revive something from the past, such as **Antony Tudor's** *Pillar of Fire*; premiere new works, such as those of **Twyla Tharp** or modern dancer **Mark Morris**; and perhaps restage one full-length ballet such as *Swan Lake*, or *Cinderella*. New York City Ballet, up to now, focuses on the ballets of **George Balanchine** and **Jerome Robbins**; recently it has begun adding works by younger choreographers such as artistic director **Peter Martins** or modern dancer **Lar Lubovitch**.

In other troupes across the country, the same holds—each season will have some premieres of new works, some revivals, or restagings of the full-length classics. These companies are usually influenced by the background of their current artistic director—the repertory may shift drastically with a change in command. For instance, San Francisco Ballet was run for some time by **Michael Smuin**, who choreographed his own pieces as well as staging those by the **Christensen Brothers** who were the original founders of the troupe. When **Helgi Tomasson** succeeded **Smuin** as director in 1985, he focused the repertory more toward the works of **Balanchine**, since Tomasson himself had danced with New York City Ballet.

Modern choreographers, unlike their ballet counterparts who created new dances within the context of an academic vocabulary, were often motivated by the need to rebel against what they believed to be the overly restrictive tenets of the classical idiom. **Isadora Duncan** was reputed to be the first in a long line of creators of "new" ways of moving. Characteristics unique to her style were the use of: long flowing gowns that freed the body for a more expansive range of movement and also revealed anatomy "honestly"; bare feet, which allowed steps to be rooted into the ground (she often performed outside on the bare earth or on a green carpet placed over the stage floor); a springy, natural motion up into the air (in lieu of the gigantic leaps and "tricks" of ballet); the ground—on her knees in supplication or lying down, either joyfully beside an imaginary stream, playing in the water with her hands, or pounding the ground with her fists in defiant anger; the great composers of classical music; and an expression of deep human emotion on all levels—grief, sorrow, joy, childlike innocence, separation, war, death, abandonment. These themes moved throughout solos that also were pure expressions of how her body intuitively responded to the music. In a sense, Isadora expanded the playful dancing that most children do naturally into a choreographed form that could be presented on the stage. Mostly she created solos for herself, though her later work included small group pieces for her students and adopted daughters.

Isadora had no systematized vocabulary for her choreography. However, she did have articulate ideas about what dancing should be, which were taught in the schools she created in Germany, France, and Russia, and later by her daughters and other followers. Her legacy is not so much a particular body of choreography or her schools, but the philosophy that dance could be a free form expression of natural ways of moving.

Martha Graham expanded on this concept while creating her own movement vocabulary. She, too, began with the idea of freeing dance from the restrictions of ballet. But her results were a definitive technique that can be taught anywhere. Two foreign companies, which maintain links with her and her New York school are the Batsheva Dance Company in Tel Aviv and the London Contemporary Dance Theatre.

Her ideas of technique translate into her choreography as seen onstage through such unique characteristics as: the *contraction*—in which the torso folds into itself at the solar plexus—a movement with a definite emotional content; flat hands with bent elbows; the forward lunge, face down, onto the floor, toes bent under to sustain the weight, the top leg folding over the supporting leg; parallel legs (instead of turned out) and flexed feet (instead of pointed); dramatic themes, especially from mythology, celebrating powerful women in history and literature and often exploring the darker side of emotions; use of sets and props integral to the dance. Graham's "dance plays" were unique combinations of dance movement and theater.

After retiring from performance, Graham often appeared for precurtain talks about dance with an eloquence reminiscent of the powerful charisma she had onstage when she performed the title roles in all her ballets. Some of her more well-known works include: *Errand into the Maze*, based on the legend of Theseus and the Minotaur—also symbolic for victory over inner fears; *Cave of the Heart*, about Jason and Medea; *Letter to the World*, in which Emily Dickinson is represented by two performers, "One Who Dances" and "One Who Speaks"; *Seraphic Dialogue*, in which Joan of Arc is portrayed by three different dancers representing three stages in the martyr's life; *Lucifer* (created in 1975 for Nureyev and Fonteyn); *Phaedra*; *Clytemnestra*; *Alcestis*; and the more lyric, pure dancing works, such as *Acrobats of God*, and *Diversion of Angels*.

Working independently as a solo dancer after leaving the Graham company, Cunningham has had his own company since 1953, with John Cage as music advisor. This collaboration has shaped profoundly the avant-garde aspects of Cunningham's notions about dance, most especially that music and dance are two separate and distinct art forms, performed simultaneously in time, and independent in nature.

Therefore, Cunningham dance is not based upon music. He choreographs and rehearses in silence. Cunningham creates a set of dance phrases, then decides what order to put them in, and in what direction they are to be danced, and by whom they should be danced, using chance operations to eliminate subjective choice on the part of the choreographer and to make dances as unpredictable as real life. This aspect of "chance" is a hallmark of Cunningham's style. In the mid-sixties, Cunningham inaugurated "Events," which were evening-long works, performed without intermission, comprised of dance phrases and segments from any number of his pieces, combined in varying order for each performance.

Recognizable stylistic elements to Cunningham's choreography are: the elongated spine; the forward *port de bras* with the back positioned low and long; the *arabesque* in which the torso elongates with the head down, as if it, too, were an extension of the spine. The arms are not always used in cor-relation with the legs, as would be found with a ballet *épaule-ment*; often the arms are stationary, *en bas*, while the legs are going all over the place. Cunningham has a predilection for high extended *développés*, often cantilevered, with the torso tilting away from the legs.

As in Graham's case the technique required to perform Cunningham's work has been codified into a rather precise movement vocabulary. Thus, while at one time revolutionary, the movement has become standardized.

The partnering in a Cunningham piece relies upon the same technical know-how as ballet, but is dispassionate in char-acter. While the dancers do relate to one another, it may simply be a matter of partners holding hands while dancing the same steps; leaning or falling into one another and then pushing away; the slight touching of a leg, arm, or face while the other dancer continues holding a pose. Like Balanchine, Cunningham is not concerned with the choreography's mean-ing. He would say that "it means I am doing this." Though it may look playful or sensual, that impression is merely the interpretation of the audience. Sometimes when a duet breaks off, one of the dancers runs offstage while the other joins an ensemble in another area of the stage. At other times, one or more dancers may remain stationary, watching the others. Cunningham incorporated the Zen concept of a "multiplicity of centers" into choreography so as to make every point on the stage equally important. For much the same reason, he considers stillness as viable as motion choreographically.

Cunningham choreographs two—and sometimes as many as four—new works a year, with a New York season every spring and a great deal of touring, especially abroad. He has also become intrigued by the ways video changes choreography and has produced several video dances.

Paul Taylor's background was more eclectic. After studying sports, he performed with Cunningham, Graham, and Pearl Lang; George Balanchine even choreographed a solo for Taylor in the ballet *Episodes*. Taylor's choreography is marked by a light spirit, usually cheerful when purely lyric and more noticeably humorous than is traditional among the "classic" modern dance choreographers. Taylor's unique movement style consists of a lot of *demi-plié* and tilted *arabesques* in which the front arm looks as if about to touch the ground. The men do their barrel turns and *jetés* low to the ground, often in a circle. There are many repetitions in Taylor work, thematic movement patterns that crop up from time to time—but not in the same way that ballet repeats once to the right and then once to the left. Taylor has also been drawn to unusual themes and odd costuming. In "*Cloven Kingdom*," for instance, his dancers begin in tuxedoes and evening gowns with formal movement and classical music. As the dance progresses, the dancers occasionally revert into animal movements as the music switches to a primitive drum ritual. Bit by bit, women appear onstage in reflecting, geometric headdresses. Taylor likes to surprise, while making his own subtle points about society. Other well-known Taylor pieces include *Airs*, performed by ABT; *Esplanade*, and *Sports and Follies*.

Of the more recent rebels, **Twyla Tharp** has made an interesting diversion—from modern back toward ballet. Like other great choreographers before her, Tharp arrived at an individual style marked by the loosening of the traditional strictures of both ballet and modern vocabulary. The influence of this style has produced countless Tharp "clones" currently trying their hand at choreography.

While she had her own company on a regular basis from 1965 until she joined American Ballet Theatre for the 1988 –89 season, Tharp has also created works for other companies, such as the Joffrey and Paris Opera Ballets. In her own way, Tharp made as controversial an impact on the dance scene as any dancer/choreographer before her. Her earlier pieces might have seemed post-modern, such as *The One Hundreds*, which consisted of a series of solos by Tharp that elaborated upon movement themes, up to 99 times, until for number 100, she is joined by 99 others who perform one movement theme each—simultaneously. But her later pieces defy categorization, such as *Eight Jelly Rolls* (music by Jelly Roll Morton), *The Bix Pieces*, and *The Fugue* (in which dancers, to an accompaniment produced by the rhythm of their feet on a miked stage, perform various discrete movement themes without an attempt to meld them together into a cohesive dance but stop in between and walk to their next position on the stage).

For the Joffrey Ballet, she choreographed *Deuce Coupe* (Beach Boys), performed by members of the Joffrey Ballet along with Tharp's own troupe *while* graffiti was being painted on the back drop. For American Ballet Theatre, Tharp choreographed *Push Comes to Shove* (Haydn). This last piece is probably most known for **Baryshnikov**'s interpretation; his career was greatly enhanced and enlarged by other Tharp ballets, such as *Sinatra Suite* and *The Little Ballet*, which were created especially for him, as well as the television special *Baryshnikov by Tharp* (1985).

She also pokes fun at ballet with little takeoffs on its language—a ballerina carefully extends her leg in *développé*, then flexes the foot improperly, falling off *pointe* and slumping her torso. Tharp usually requires the dancers in her own company to wear jazz shoes because of the speed they allow, especially for turns. While much of her odd, or at times, quirky choreography looks as if it must be improvised due to its flip and casual air, it actually requires perfect timing and structure so that, according to Tharp, "the dancers don't kill each other at those speeds." Tharp ballets, for certain, are funny. Just when the movement appears to be serious and beautiful, she throws in a fluke. In *Push Comes to Shove*, for instance, Baryshnikov does a series of turns, goes off-balance (planned, not a mistake as it might be in ballet), and keeps turning on flat foot, his head—instead of spotting—going with his body, as if he were either confused or looking for someone.

A word about choreographic intent. Shoes are chosen to fit the needs of the choreographer's technical demands. Bare feet will hug the ground better for low movement and balances; technique slippers or JAZZ SLIPPERS (flat soles with long laces up the calves), or JAZZ SHOES (which look a bit like lightweight street oxfords, lacing across the top) allow easier turning and faster moving. The *pointe* shoe is specifically for work on the toes, allows for demonspeed turns, and elongates the look of the rest of the body. While at one time the shoe defined which style of dance, now it is the choreographer's choice, whether in modern or ballet, jazz or show dancing.

Tharp's foray into the classical ballet halls is not that unusual anymore. **Laura Dean** was commissioned to do two ballets for the Joffrey, and Lar Lubovitch premiered *Rhapsody in Blue* for the 1988 New American Music Festival presented by New York City Ballet.

Regardless of the company, and whether in the modern or classical idiom, what all these choreographers have in common is the creative process of putting together movement for the human body. No matter what milieu, what intent, what country, what era, what vocabulary, what style—choreographing is creating. With or without a divine spark of inspiration, the dance has to be made. Sometimes there is a deadline of a performance date; sometimes the deadline is because of union rules that allow only so much time for the choreographer to work with the dancers; sometimes the deadline is a residency or a tour or money. But whatever the motivating force, like any creative art, choreography boils down to a single moment which Jerome Robbins described as "just go in the studio and do it."

TECHNICAL ASPECTS:

BEHIND THE SCENES

W hat goes on behind the scenes is what makes the stage performance happen. The cast of characters who are never seen are also perhaps the least well understood. Let's take a look at who does what in the dark areas beyond the wings.

First of all, the dance is designed many months—and sometimes years—before it goes into production. A PRODUCTION is the total of everything required to get a dance produced on stage. Otherwise, dance would simply be choreography performed in a studio. The **designers** include the choreographer, who works out the total vision for the dance in collaboration with lighting, scenery, and costume designers. (Sometimes there is also a prop designer, although usually this role is handled by the set designer.)

After their discussions, designs are created for both sets and costumes, usually in scale renderings, which are then sent to carpentry and costume shops to be executed. When the work is completed, the costumes are delivered to the wardrobe master and wardrobe mistress. (There is generally one costume head for each sex.) The sets are turned over to the carpentry crew, who are known collectively as GRIPS.

Although specifics may change according to size and budget of the dance company, the typical minimum would be one **technical director**, a **stage manager**, a **head carpenter**, **head electrician**, and **wardrobe head**. The employees who work under these heads are the **hired crew**. A company may hire a crew of fifteen one night, and then hire double that number for a more technically complex dance the next. According to these specifications, a company turns in what is known as a YELLOW CARD with their crew request to the union. A resident dance company can generally expect to be sent the same crew for each season.

Crews must be augmented in productions requiring elaborate set changes. For example, San Francisco Ballet's *Nutcracker* requires three times the number of personnel as most ballets because of all the scenery, props, and quick scene changes, as well as magical effects.

When on tour, only the heads, or company employees, go along with the dancers. A different crew is hired in each city, which the heads, according to union rules, can only direct. Crew heads teach the local crew and supervise, but generally they are not allowed to touch anything in a tour house. An exception to this rule would be when the company has brought their own lighting board and lights—then they can hang the lights themselves and run the light board, which governs those lights only. There will still have to be a local crew running the local theater's lighting board.

As for other tour headaches, ninety-nine percent of the time a light cannot be hung exactly in the same place in a tour theater that it can at home. This may be due to such a simple problem as different architecture—a pole may be placed in a strategic location or the wall of the tour theater may curve at a different angle. On tour, crews have about twenty-four hours to prepare a theater. Generally, they arrive at 8 A.M. and have a performance that night at 8 P.M., so there's not enough time to deal with all the differences in that theater. As the stage manager for San Francisco Ballet put it, "You have to make do and you have to do it *fast*."

The **wardrobe crew** maintain the costumes. This requires making sure that every piece of every costume is in the appropriate dressing room; that every dancer gets whatever he or she needs to dance his or her role—everything, that is, except shoes, which are the dancer's personal responsibility. (Principal dancers can go through two pairs of *pointe* shoes a day.) If the dancer's shoes must be dyed to match, then it is his or her own job to get those shoes to wardrobe to be spray-painted before the performance.

Wardrobe also does laundry and keeps costumes clean throughout the run of any given ballet. This may include altering a costume between matinee and evening performances, if it is to be worn by a different dancer in a different cast. Wardrobe also acts as DRESSERS to assist dancers with quick costume changes or costumes that are difficult to get into, such as tutus, which fasten tightly up the back. Wardrobe CALL (or arrival time) is usually 7 P.M., since the crew needs to prepare and deliver costumes to dressing rooms.

The **carpentry crew**, known as CARPS or GRIPS, are divided into two categories: those who work the DECK, or main floor of the stage, and pull something by hand; and those who work the RAIL or fly gallery, and pull FLIES, or ropes connected to scenery and lighting pipes hung high over the stage.

This crew of HOUSE CARPENTERS are different from the SHOP CARPENTERS, who are responsible for building the sets. Their job is complete once the sets are delivered to the theater. House carpenters only do actual carpentry work if something breaks during production and needs fixing.

An **electrician** handles anything that plugs into a wall socket, which includes lights, follow spots, any pyrotechnics needed for special effects, and electrified props. For instance, if a prop is battery operated, the carpenters build it and the electricians put in the batteries. This crew is primarily responsible for carrying out the specifications of the lighting designer.

The **prop crew** handle pretty much everything to do with the floor—clearing the stage after a production, setting out *barres* for company class onstage the next day, rolling up the floor, cleaning the floor, setting up chairs for the orchestra.

About a week before a show is due to OPEN, or premiere, the **stage manager** begins watching rehearsals from the HOUSE, or audience, with the choreographer and lighting designer. A stage manager can either be a full-time employee of the dance company, or hired for a particular show, what is known as a CONTRACT STAGE MANAGER. During these rehearsals, the stage manager SETS the cues by marking where they will be called in either a score of the music for the ballet or, as is the case with American Ballet Theatre, on TRACK SHEETS which are diagrams of stage movements by the dancers. Sometimes the cue is musical, for instance, a light changes on a particular note; at other times, the cue is visual, such as when a particular dancer finishes a *pirouette* downstage right.

During these meetings, the **lighting designer** will see where the set units are sitting and then decide where to hang lights, how to focus them, and what color the lights will be. These specifications are then carried out by the electricians, or **lighting crew**.

At this time, the stage manager also notifies the crew as to how many hours they'll be needed in the house to prepare for the new ballet. (Sometimes the stage manager also plans the full production schedule, called CALENDARING. For instance, "In April, we'll build *Nutcracker* . . . Next Monday morning at 8 A.M. we go in to hang lights.")

Lights are divided into HOUSE, or those which illumine the audience portion of the theater, and STAGE lights, which light the stage and backstage areas. The former are controlled by a house board, which is run by a house electrician, who controls all the lights over the audience.

Stage lights are controlled from a LIGHT BOOTH, which is generally located behind the first balcony. This booth may be divided into two rooms—the light board and **light board operator** are located in one; the front-of-house follow spots are in the other. FOLLOW SPOTS do what their name implies—follow a dancer about the stage. Another type of follow spot, located over the stage, lights from directly above the dancer instead of from in front of the dancer. Front-of-house follow spots tend to be FLAT ON, meaning that, because they are located at stage level, the intensity of the light shines directly into the dancer's eyes. These have a tendency to blind the dancers, thereby preventing them from being able to SPOT for turns (meaning here, to fix an object with the eye while the body is turning in order to maintain balance). Another disadvantage to front-of-house follow spots is that they put a big ring on the set behind the dancer.

Stage lights are either above the stage and mounted on pipes from electrical bridges, or they are mounted in the wings on booms. BRIDGES over the dancers' heads are wide enough for electricians to walk across them, eliminating the need to refocus or change a light by bringing the entire pipe down. (A PIPE is what the lights are mounted on.)

Lights in the wings are called BOOMS. Booms are vertical pipes mounted either on a stand or on wheels. These vertically mounted lights, which are also known as LADDERS, shine from the sides, rather than from the top and down on the dancers.

Different ways to light a set, or stage, include: FRONT LIGHTS, or those hung in the house, which shine directly onto the stage; SIDE LIGHT, from the booms in the wings; BACK LIGHT, from behind the stage; AREA LIGHT, from up above the stage (these light the nine areas of the stage as derived from traditional theatrical terms: downstage right, downstage center, downstage left, etcetera); WASH, lighting that covers the entire stage and is nonspecific; and SPECIAL, a light that is focused on a particular part of the set or dancer for emphasis.

Sets for a production consist of either three-dimensional SCENERY, or whatever sits directly on the stage, and two-dimensional DROPS, which are flown from above the stage where they are hung on BATTENS, or pipes similar to those for the lights.

The fly gallery is located above the stage where the sets hang. The GRID is that space itself, between sixty and eighty feet above the stage floor in most houses, or the GRIDWORK of pulleys and ropes. These ropes are handled by the grips who work the rail. The RAIL is a set of LINES, or ropes, which run along a side wall of the backstage area. Every line connects to a pipe overhead where is hung either a scenery drop, or lights. A rope will pull either on and off stage sideways, or up and down.

Ropes also control most **curtains**. The main, or PROSCENIUM, CURTAIN is the one which goes up and down between ballets, and that is often electronically controlled. However, the BOW CURTAIN, or the one which splits in the middle for dancers to come out onto the apron for their bows, is pulled by ropes. (In many theaters, however, the proscenium and the bow curtain are one and the same.) Other curtains include SCRIMS, which are opaque if lit from the front and transparent if lighted behind; a PLASTIC PROJECTION SCREEN, usually at the very back of the stage; a BOC, or BLACKOUT CURTAIN, which is used to help the audience suspend their disbelief—it is lowered whenever a scene change needs to take place while the action continues. There are also legs in the wings: the WINGS are the areas through which the dancers exit and enter; the curtains, usually black velour, that separate the wings, are called LEGS.

To keep the complicated system of lines and pulleys organized, there is a RAIL SHEET, which identifies every line and its corresponding pipe. The head carpenter determines what will be hung on each of the pipes; a label, or TAG, will be placed near that line designating it as such—for instance, "#3 border."

Tech rehearsals were originally instituted so that the technical crew would have a chance to run through their cues. Technical rehearsals are also an opportunity for the choreographer and designers to see the final effect and decide what changes they want to make. This is their chance to see how the lights, costumes, and scenery look with the dancers. During tech rehearsal, the choreographer sees what the lighting designer has come up with and each may decide something like, "I want more blue on that dancer," or, "I want the sky more red." This is also a time for the designers to tell the stage manager when they want the scene changes to occur: for instance, "During this music I want the sky drop to fall." Generally, designers change their minds right up to the opening curtain.

A **dress rehearsal** refers to a run-through with dancers dressed in full costumes and makeup. However, if the costumes are unusual, such as very long skirts, a huge headpiece, or a stiff tutu, the dancers may rehearse in their costumes ahead of time in the studio to get accustomed to them. The dress rehearsal is actually the only time cast, crew, and orchestra get a full run-through together before the performance, because the tech rehearsal usually involves a lot of stopping and starting for changes and there is no orchestra then. Generally, the tempi have been worked out beforehand in studio rehearsals, but quite often the dancers have not heard the music with full orchestra before this time.

When it finally comes time for a performance, all crew check in to the theater at HALF HOUR, or thirty minutes before curtain. Technical crews work different hours from the performers. They generally work eight hours for LOAD-IN, or setting up the theater either during tour or for the opening of every new ballet. After that, crew are called for tech and dress rehearsals at half hour. When a performance is over, crew members fly all scenery up before leaving the theater or they load up scenery for the next theater on the tour.

Their backstage jobs are CALLED during the performance by the stage manager. The stage manager does exactly what the title suggests, "manages" the stage. In a performance, even the dancers defer to the stage manager. Usually he or she stands at one side of the stage, nearest the apron, in front of a console with a headset on, giving directions to people in various locations.

Referred to as CALLING a show, the stage manager calls the cues. This is how the stage manager orchestrates what's going on behind the scenes. There are numerous lighting and scene changes that take place during a dance itself. CUES to make these changes are given by the stage manager to the crews, in their various locations backstage. WARNINGS precede cues by thirty seconds. Light cues and rail cues are either numbered or lettered. For instance, "rail cue B" may involve moving five pieces of scenery by eight crewmen. The cue is still just "rail cue B" and it's up to the head carpenter to determine which of his or her crew does what and where.

It is the stage manager who first calls half hour. Over the public address system will be heard something like: "Ladies and Gentlemen, this is your half-hour call." The next call is fifteen minutes, then ten, then, at five minutes, this is heard over the backstage p.a. system: "Ladies and Gentlemen, the call is ONSTAGE for ballet so-and-so. Crew to the stage." If there is live music with an orchestra, the stage manager will also say at this time: "Ladies and Gentlemen of the orchestra,

to the orchestra pit, please. Maestro so-and-so to the stage."
The reason to call the conductor to the stage manager's side
is in case there is a request for a late curtain. Sometimes the
curtain is held five minutes because of a long line at WILL
CALL (people waiting to pick up prepaid tickets), or audience
waiting to be seated by ushers, or a change in casts.

At two minutes, the backstage goes into what is termed
PRESET. The conductor is sent by the stage manager down to
wait at the entrance to the pit. The first lighting cue is called;
all scenery is in place. Dancers are called to "Places." Houselights are called to "half."

And then the performance call: "Houselights down—go.
Main curtain up—go. Follow spot to center girls—go." And
the performance is underway.

Headphones and a p.a. system are used where possible for
the crew to communicate with one another. For those crew
located where no headsets are possible, or those waiting behind
the scenery onstage who cannot hear the verbal cues from the
stage manager, CUE LIGHTS are used. Colored light bulbs are
located along the sides of the backstage area where appropriate
crew members can see them. The WARNING—or 30 seconds
—is given when the cue lights go on. All crew members then
keep their eyes on the lights—the moment they go off is the
signal to "go" and they begin moving the scenery for the next
scene.

Someone from the technical crew may sit or stand at the
back of the house to watch for trouble. For instance, during
the San Francisco Ballet's performance of *Nutcracker* one year,
a prop fell and got caught on a curtain in the wings. None of
the dancers noticed because they were busy dancing; the tech
crew were all backstage so they couldn't see it. Thank heaven
the tech director was in the house, observed the calamity, and
dashed backstage to make amends.

When the last bow is over, the stage manager calls, "House-lights to full—go. Work lights on—go. Save the board—go," which means turn off the stage lights.

The separate backstage crews must work together as a cohesive unit, or all those myriad responsibilities would jam up on top of one another. One of the biggest backstage headaches is traffic—wardrobe, dancers, lighting crew, all crowding the wings at once. Duties are carefully assigned so that each person has a specific job in a specific place. Cooperation among the crews, and between tech crews and performers, is vital. The old adage, "There's no business like show business," is most obvious backstage, where every individual, from dancers to crew, is part of a group effort which becomes the final performance.

ENDNOTE

While there is no substitute for the visual—and visceral—immediacy of dance, the following sections are designed to lead you into that experience armed with information that will broaden your ability to see. If there were one thing only that you glean from reading this book, I would like it to be the ability to trust your own judgment.

All the reading in the world cannot quite compare with what happens to you when the curtain rises. And yet, it is my hope that this book has given you a sense of what to expect, of what it takes to bring that performance to life, of the history that developed the artform, of what goes into choreographing or becoming a dancer. Most important, you should have acquired an ability to discern: not just the difference between what is good and bad, or difficult and easy, but also which types of dance and styles of choreography you prefer.

George Balanchine has been known to suggest that the audience should never analyze; they should just watch. With this book as your companion, and the familiarity you'll gain simply from watching dance, I can guarantee a richer audience experience that may grow into a lifetime of performance attendance.

TICKET BUYER'S GUIDE

If you were to go by the price of tickets, you might assume the best seats in the theater were in the orchestra and the boxes. For some people and some theaters, this is probably true. But I would like to suggest that the best seat depends upon what you want to see.

Your first consideration when choosing a seat for viewing dance is whether the piece is something you want to see up close and intimately—such as a small modern dance company—or, as with a full-length classical ballet, do you want a more distant perspective that will allow you to see full stage patterns of the entire dance troupe. While it can be fun to be so close as to see them sweat, you may also be missing the formations of the lines of the corps de ballet which are an important part of the choreography in something like *Swan Lake* or *Giselle*.

A good compromise is usually the back of the orchestra section, where there is some distance from the stage but also the advantage of not being so high up that you lose an intimacy with the performers. Beware the orchestra of a theater with which you aren't familiar, however. Check first to see how the floor is raked; rows near the front may be lower than the stage, effectively cutting off the dancers' feet and making you crane your neck upward. In addition, you may find that the rows are not staggered, meaning that the patron in front of you will block your view. The more raked the seating, the better your chances of seeing clearly.

On your first visit to a new theater, play it safe and sit the first level up from the main floor. At intermission, take note of the theater's seating arrangements for future visits, marking the rows which are raked sufficiently to keep your view open from others, yet not so close that you risk missing part of the dancer's body. Also, beware of sitting too far to either side; as much as one-third of the action may be blocked.

Occasionally, these "partial view" seats are okay. If you are particularly interested in seeing a *pas de deux* or solo piece, for instance, the closer you are physically to the stage, the less of it you'll see on the side you're sitting, but you'll certainly see the center stage action quite clearly. For some ensemble works, or when the scenery is not a consideration, close and to the side of the stage can be quite nice. (Close to the stage in the *center* is usually terrible. While the angle resulting from a side position will prevent heads from blocking your view, in the center someone may be smack in front of you; the conductor's arms may cut across a dancer at a most inopportune time; and if the house is not raked steeply down front, you'll be looking UP all evening.)

Becoming familiar with the theater is, in all cases, the safest bet. Usually the first tier above the orchestra is the most preferred because it gives an over-all picture of the stage, for large ensemble works and corps patterns, but is not so far away that you can't see clearly the individual dancers.

While I happen to enjoy the grander scale perspective many balcony seats offer when it comes to a full-length ballet, in some theaters the balconies are hung way at the back of the house. In this case, I feel so far away that the action seems almost to take place in another country. If you like viewing individual dancers through powerful binoculars, this approach can still work; remember, however, that you'll lose some of the action on the rest of the stage while peeking through your lenses. In general, I recommend being further away for dances with large companies, or story ballets, and closer for an evening of *pas de deux* or to see a particular soloist or a smaller ensemble.

As for what kind of dance performance is best to start with, some feel that story ballets are the most accessible for the beginner. On the other hand, these often contain lengthy sections with little dancing and much drama, which can seem tedious if it's the dancing, as opposed to the story, you've come to see. Instead, try an evening of *divertissements*; you'll see a little of everything—and usually the best dancers the company has to offer. If you are not sure you'll like modern dance, try, for starters, seeing a ballet company that offers contemporary work along with the classical repertory. Should classical ballet bore you, try a contemporary ballet company first before plunging into the more traditional fare.

When at all in doubt about which company, which repertory or which dancer to buy a ticket for, refer back to the listed characteristics in the chapters on choreographers, modern dance, and history. These should give you a brief idea of the type of movement you're likely to see in each company. Or, you might just take a plunge and see a company you've never heard of and which isn't mentioned in this book. But remember to keep your eyes—and your mind—open.

Refer to the checklist in "How to Watch Dance" (Part One) for qualities that are seen in any dance and note what you like and what you don't. If the performance disappoints you, you'll at least know what or who you *don't* want to see next time. Undoubtedly, though, there'll be something in the evening's work that appealed to you; if not the choreography, then a particular dancer; if not the company, then perhaps a choreographer whose work you can see in another ensemble.

Any performance can be an enjoyable experience, depending upon how you approach it and what you expect. Even after years and years of viewing dance, I always find something new or exciting in every performance I see. You just have to look.

SUGGESTED
READING

There are some "bibles" that I would never be without. If you buy only a few books to increase your audience enjoyment, make them these:

1. Encyclopedias and dictionaries.

Here you can look up the name of a dancer, a ballet, a dance company, a composer, and dance terms. My suggestions are:

The Concise Oxford Dictionary of Ballet, revised edition. Horst Koegler (Oxford University Press: London, 1982).

A Dictionary of Ballet, third edition. G. B. L. Wilson (Theatre Arts Books: New York, 1974).

Dictionary of Modern Ballet. Selma Jeanne Cohen, editor (Tudor Publishing Co.: New York, 1959). (Selma Jeanne Cohen is also in the process of producing an international encyclopedia of dance—watch for it!) Especially interesting because of the more detailed entries about dancers who were current at the time of its publication.

2. Ballet Stories.

My all-time favorite (but difficult to obtain) is *Balanchine's New Complete Stories of the Great Ballets*. George Balanchine and Francis Mason, editors (Doubleday: New York, 1968). Here is where you can look up the name of any ballet mentioned in my book for a complete description of the story, movement, and performance. Balanchine's volume offers several books in one: Part One—stories of the great ballets; Part Two—How to Enjoy Ballet; the other nine sections cover such topics as a brief history of ballet, chronology of ballet, ballet for children, careers in ballet, notes on choreography, selected reading, glossary of dance terms, and Balanchine talking about how he became a dancer and choreographer. Just about everything you need in one book!

(There is also a paperback version, *101 Stories of the Great Ballets*, by George Balanchine and Francis Mason (Anchor Books: New York, 1975), containing only the ballet stories and not the glossary of terms and other sections.)

Walter Terry, who was dance critic of *Saturday Review*, wrote—among many other books—*Ballet Guide* (Dodd Mead, New York, 1982). Background, listings, credits, and descriptions of more than five hundred of the world's major ballets. (Very interesting Introduction, with good sections called "The History of Ballet" and "On Looking at the Ballet," and a glossary of terms.)

3. Technique.

Technical Manual and Dictionary of Classical Ballet. Gail Grant (Dover Publications: New York, 1967). With illustrations by the author, this little paperback gives pronunciation of French dance terms and describes the primary steps in careful, detailed, and understandable language.

For more extensive descriptions, such as all the different arm positions named by the different schools (Cecchetti, French, Russian, Lifar, etc.), with illustrations of steps, see:

A *Dictionary of Ballet Terms*. Leo Kersley and Janet Sinclair (Adams & Charles Black: London, 1953).

The Classic Ballet (Alfred A. Knopf: New York, 1952), with "Historical Development" by Lincoln Kirstein and "Basic Technique and Terminology" by Muriel Stuart, describes how basic technique steps are executed. Illustrations by Carlus Dyer indicate the progression of the movements.

Basic Principles of Classical Ballet. Agrippina Vaganova (Dover Publications: New York, 1969). This book illustrates Russian ballet technique.

4. History.

The best short and easily readable history is Jack Anderson's *Ballet and Modern Dance: A Concise History* (Princeton Book Company: Princeton, N.J., 1986). With 198 interesting pages, the book includes in each chapter a "Related Readings" section with writings from historical figures pertinent to that period. In addition, there is also a bibliography for further reading in each area and—best of all—"Short Profiles," or quick paragraphs, describing all important figures in the history of dance.

5. Criticism.

Several illustrious and lucid dance critics have published collections of their reviews which illuminate the dance-watching experience. These collections reveal the way in which critics watch dance as well as specifics they look for and comment upon. Reviews are also, in their own way, a history of dance in performance.

Looking at the Dance. Edwin Denby (Horizon Press: New York, 1968). The first section of this volume, "Meaning in Ballet," contains essays very helpful in how to watch, most especially "How to Judge a Dancer." Noteworthy also is the final essay, "The Critic."

Also by Denby: *Dancers, Buildings and People in the Streets* (Popular Library: New York, 1979) and *Dance Writings* (Alfred A. Knopf: New York, 1986). If he is all you ever read, you will have read the best.

Arlene Croce, critic for *The New Yorker* and the founder of the periodical *Ballet Review*, has also published collections of her writings, *Afterimages* (Random House: New York, 1977), *Going to the Dance* (Knopf: New York, 1982), *Dancing on My Mind* (Knopf: New York, 1987), and *Sight Lines* (Knopf: New York, 1987), as well as *The Fred Astaire and Ginger Rogers Book* (Dutton: New York, 1987).

Deborah Jowitt, former dancer and critic for New York's *Village Voice*, has published her collected reviews, *Dance Beat* (Marcel Dekker: New York, 1977) and *Dance In Mind* (David Godine: Boston, 1985), as well as *Time and the Dancing Image* (Morrow: New York, 1987), which contains photographs of modern dancers in performance which illustrate clearly how their techniques varied and how their choreography looks in performance. Jowitt's premise is to discuss how the social times in which dancers developed affected their art.

Marcia Siegel, who has also published her collected reviews —*At the Vanishing Point* (Saturday Review Press: New York, 1972) and *Watching the Dance Go By* (Houghton Mifflin: Boston, 1977)—has also written *Shapes of Change: Images of American Dance* (University of California Press: Berkeley, 1985), in which she discusses specific dances of Doris Humphrey,

Martha Graham, George Balanchine, José Limón, Paul Taylor, Merce Cunningham, Jerome Robbins, Twyla Tharp, and other seminal figures in American dance. (Also has a terrific bibliography, by topic.)

GLOSSARY

ADAGIO As in music, the opposite of ALLEGRO, or a slower tempo. *Adagio* (or *adage*, in French) is also a set of practice exercises in class, consisting of DÉVELOPPÉS, EXTENSIONS, and balances.

ADJUSTING Making allowances for not finishing a step exactly in proper position by moving the body or feet slightly.

À LA SECONDE To the side.

ALIGNMENT The way in which various parts of the dancer's body are in line with one another while the dancer is moving.

ALLEGRO From the musical term, this refers to quick or lively movements, such as all steps of *élévation* and *batterie*.

APRON The section of the stage between the proscenium curtain and the orchestra pit; the area in front of the curtain where dancers take their final bows.

ARABESQUE A pose in which the working leg is extended with a straight knee directly behind the body (both height of leg and position of the arms are variable).

ARABESQUE PENCHÉE A version of the *arabesque* in which the leg is lifted in degrees, as high as a vertical in the air, with the torso bending forward in opposition to it, like a teeter-totter.

ARTISTIC DIRECTOR The overall head of the dance company; sometimes, also the choreographer.

À TERRE (see Par terre)

ATTACK How a dancer begins a movement.

ATTITUDE A pose modeled after the statue of the winged Mercury by Bologna in which the working leg is extended behind the body with the knee bent. Can also be held in front of the body, *attitude en avant*. Most attitudes are performed with the thigh and the calf on the same plane, although Soviet attitudes are known for extending the calf much higher, with the foot pointed toward the head.

BALLET MASTER The person responsible for overseeing rehearsals, teaching company class, and training the dancers.

BALLET SLIPPER The technique shoe worn by men in performance and by women in rehearsal and class; it is soft, made either of leather or canvas, and held on the foot with elastic sewn across the instep.

BARRE A round rail attached to the wall horizontally, about 3½ feet above the floor, for dancers to hold during the first half of technique class; also used for stretching the legs, by placing the feet or legs on it. For companies on tour, portable *barres*, on legs, are set up on stage for class.

BASIC POSITIONS The five positions of the arms and feet so called because they are the basis for all steps in the vocabulary of the classic dance.

BATTERIE "Beats" refers to various steps in which the feet or legs strike each other, either one beating against the other or in which the two feet beat together; for example, *brisé*, *cabriole*, *entrechat*.

BOURRÉE A series of swift, traveling steps done *sur les pointes* so quickly that separation between the dancer's legs is not discernible. Usually done in fifth position (crossed); may also be executed in first position parallel. (Technically, *"pas de bourrée couru"* or running; among dancers, usually called just *bourrées*, in the plural, since most forms of *pas de bourrée* employ a changing of the feet.)

BOX The area of the POINTE SHOE on which the ballerina stands.

BREAKING IN A process individual to every ballerina in which the POINTE SHOE is softened and prepared for wearing onstage.

CALLED Refers to how cues are given by the stage manager for the crew and dancers during a performance.

CHAÎNÉS Literally, "chains"; rapid turns executed on the POINTES or DEMI-POINTES, either in a straight line or a circle.

CHARACTER SHOE A heeled shoe worn in folk, or "character" dances in full-length ballets.

CHEATING Adjusting a movement so that it looks better during performance but is not technically correct.

CHOREOGRAPHY From Greek, "dance writing"; the steps of a dance as put together for performance, or the art of composing dances.

CLASSICAL (or "academic" dance) Refers to the lexicon of dance as taught in the original academies; also used in reference to ballets as created during the Imperial Russian days, such as *The Sleeping Beauty, Nutcracker, Swan Lake*; also refers to a style of performing that was developed over the years from France, Italy, Denmark, and Russia, or the kind of dancing that comes from that style.

CORPS DE BALLET Literally, the "body of the ballet," or the chorus; the dancers who stand behind the principals, forming a stage picture with their poses; also, all those members of a dance company who are not designated as soloists or principals.

COURTESY OF Refers to having borrowed sets or costumes for a production from another company.

CURTAIN CALL Acknowledgment of applause with bows or curtsies when the ballet is completed.

DEMI-POINTE **(also, *half pointe*)** On the ball of the foot, or half toe.

DESIGNED Refers to the creation of sets, costumes, and lights; artistic creation, not construction.

DÉVELOPPÉ From the French, "to develop or unfold"; a gradual extending of the leg from the floor, the foot passing along the knee of the supporting leg (PASSÉ) and unfolding either to the front, the side, or the back.

DIVERTISSEMENT A virtuoso dance taken from a larger work.

DROPS Two-dimensional scenery that is hung.

ÉLÉVATION The ability to get up into the air and remain there long enough to perform various movements or poses.

EN ARRIÈRE Backward.

EN AVANT Forward.

EN BAS Low, usually used in reference to an arm position, as fifth position *en bas*.

EN HAUT High; used to indicate when the arms are raised over the head.

EN L'AIR Literally, "in the air"; refers to steps performed in the air, either JETÉS, *sautés* (jumps), or BATTERIES, or to a leg that is in the air, as during an EXTENSION.

ENSEMBLE The ability to dance together in unison; also, a group of dancers.

ENTRECHAT A "beating" movement in which the feet criss-cross one another around the ankles in the air with the legs straight. These are designated by number to indicate how many exchanges of the feet take place, such as *entrechat quatre* (four) or *entrechat huit* (eight).

ÉPAULEMENT Placement of the shoulders; how the shoulders, neck, and head move in relation particularly to the arms and also the rest of the body.

EXTENSION Raising the leg to a straightened position with the foot very high above the ground; the ability to lift and hold the leg in position off the ground.

FINGER TURNS In PAS DE DEUX, the ballerina is supported for her PIROUETTES by holding the index or middle finger of the danseur's hand as it is held over her head.

FIRST CAST The dancers originally taught the choreography and those who generally perform it; second cast are often stand-ins for the first cast or scheduled to dance less frequently.

FISH DIVE (**Pas de Poisson**) A lift in which the ballerina is balanced by the danseur in an inverted position, with her legs up and behind his body, her head near the ground and bent back, forming an upward arc with the rest of her torso.

FOLLOW SPOTS Large, bright lights that "follow" a leading dancer around the stage, making him or her stand out from the other dancers.

FOUETTÉ From *fouetter*, "to whip"; a PIROUETTE in which the working leg whips in and out from PASSÉ to DÉVELOPPÉ À LA SECONDE.

GRAND JETÉ From *jeter*, "to throw"; a leap from one leg to the other, in which the working leg is kicked or thrown away from the body and into the air; the pose achieved in the air differs, as does the direction the *jeté* takes. (Gail Grant's dictionary of technical ballet terms lists thirty-seven types of *jetés*.) By way of contrast, the term *sauté* (or jump) is used in dance to indicate that a step is done with a jump, such as *sauté en arabesque*, *échappé sauté*, etc.

GRAND JETÉ EN TOURNANT In this leap the dancer turns halfway in midair to land facing the direction in which the movement started. (Also called **tour jeté** by some teachers.)

GUESTING Dancing with a company other than one's home troupe.

HALF HOUR The STAGE MANAGER's call thirty minutes before curtain; also, the time that all performers and CREW must report to the theater.

ISADORABLES Young girls adopted by Isadora Duncan as her daughters, with whom she performed and who taught her choreography after her death.

JUDSON DANCE THEATER A group of artists who assembled in the 1960s in order to create a new way of treating modern dance as nonacademic; named after the church in Greenwich

Village where they met, they often performed in unusual spaces, such as art galleries, parks, and lofts, sometimes with untrained dancers and often in sneakers.

KINESTHETIC AWARENESS Feeling the dance movement of others in one's own muscles.

LIFTS A part of PAS DE DEUX in which one dancer is lifted off the ground by the other.

LINE The arrangement of head, shoulders, arms, torso, and legs while dancing.

MARKING Walking through, or indicating the steps with the hands, instead of dancing; used in rehearsal.

MASTER CLASSES Technique classes taught by well-known dancers, often to dancers unfamiliar with the teacher's technique.

MINIMALISTS Modern dancers who pared movement down to repeatable basic phrases.

MOUNT The process necessary for getting a ballet into performance, including all production preparations.

MUSCLE MEMORY The way in which most choreography is remembered by dancers.

NEOCLASSICISM A term coined to denote that form and technique of dancing which came after classicism; often used in reference to George Balanchine, although he never used this expression to describe his work.

PAR TERRE (or *à terre*) On the ground; used especially when there is a need to differentiate between movements done both *par terre* and EN L'AIR, such as *ronds de jambe*, or circles of the leg.

PAS A dance "step," as *pas seul* (dance for one), *pas de deux* (dance for two), *pas de chat* (cat-like step), *pas de bourrée*.

PAS DE BOURRÉE (see BOURRÉE)

PAS DE DEUX Literally, "a step for two"; referring to the codified form which is choreographed in many classical ballets, consisting of *entrée* and ADAGIO, a variation for each dancer, and a coda; it also is used to refer to any section of a dance performed by two dancers together.

PASSÉ A "passing" position, usually part of DÉVELOPPÉ, in which the foot passes by the knee of the supporting leg. When this position is held, as in PIROUETTES, with the foot of the working leg resting against the knee of the supporting leg, it is known as *retiré*.

PIQUÉ From *piquer*, "to prick"; stepping directly onto the *half pointe* or *pointe* of the supporting leg with the knee straight; can be done in many different poses, such as *arabesque piquée* or as a PIROUETTE.

PIROUETTE French, "to whirl or spin"; a *tour*, or turn, on one foot that can be executed outward (*en dehors*, away from the body) or inward (*en dedans*, toward the body).

PIT The area of the theater where the orchestra sits.

PLIÉ A bending of the knees; can be *grand*, as in exercises done at the BARRE in class for warm-up; or *demi-plié*, as when the dancer is preparing for a jump off the ground.

POINTE Dancing on the toes, or *sur les pointes*.

POINTE SHOE The pink satin slipper in which the ballerina dances on the tips of her toes.

POLE LIFT A one-handed lift in which the ballerina is held above the danseur's head as if seated in the palm of his hand.

PORT DE BRAS Carriage of the arms; refers to specific arm positions and also movements of the arms, such as *grand port de bras*, which is a series of movements practiced in class like the basic steps of the feet.

POST-MODERN DANCE A term coined in the 1960s by those who wished to create movement outside the influences of any of the then-traditional modern dance pioneers, such as Cunningham, Graham, Humphrey, Limón, and Taylor.

PREPARATION The steps that aid a dancer in performing a movement; for instance, a *demi-plié* is usually a preparation for a JETÉ, and fourth position with *demi-plié* is generally the preparation for a PIROUETTE.

PRESENTER The person or organization responsible for bringing the dance company to the stage in performance (in other words, who pays for the performances).

PROMENADE An ADAGIO movement in which the dancer pivots completely around on one foot while maintaining a pose with the working leg. In PAS DE DEUX, a promenade is performed with the ballerina maintaining a pose *sur la pointe*, while the danseur walks around her.

PROSCENIUM The section of the stage that sets it apart from the audience, or HOUSE.

RAKING The slant of the house upward from the stage to the lobby.

RÉGISSEUR The organizer of rehearsals, studios, casts, and daily company nitty-gritty.

RELEVÉ From *relever*, "to lift again"; raising the foot from a flat, standing position onto either *half pointe* (or *demi-pointe*) or full *pointe*.

REPERTORY, REPERTOIRE All the ballets currently performed by a dance company.

RESTAGED Refers to a new staging of an original production, either with new choreography or new sets and costumes, or both.

RETIRÉ (see PASSÉ)

REVIVAL The presentation of a ballet once again which has not been in active REPERTOIRE.

ROMANTIC ERA A period from about 1820 to 1870 in which ballet was characterized primarily by supernatural subject matter (*La Sylphide*, *Giselle*), long white tutus, dancing on the *pointes*, and theatrical innovations that permitted the dimming of the houselights for theatrical illusion.

RUN The period of time a certain ballet is being performed.

SCRIM A curtain that is translucent when a light is in front of it, so it can be used for scenery, and transparent when light is behind it, so that dancers can be seen through it.

SEASON The time during which a company is actively performing.

SET ON A term used to describe when a choreographer teaches his or her steps to a certain dancer or a certain company; particularly refers to when movements are specifically created with a certain dancer's qualities or body type in mind.

SHOULDER LIFT A lift in which the ballerina is seated on the danseur's shoulder.

SPOTTING Focusing the eyes on one point in the distance in order to keep balance while turning.

STAGED BY Refers to having a ballet SET ON a particular company by an individual.

SUPPORTING LEG The leg upon which the dancer is balancing.

TECH REHEARSAL A run-through for checking lights, scenery, and costumes, primarily for the CREW to rehearse their CUES.

TOUR EN L'AIR A complete turn in the air, the body in a straight line, with the feet together, toes pointed, beginning and ending in fifth position; these can be performed double or triple, meaning two or three complete revolutions while in the air.

TURNOUT Rotating the leg outward from the hip such that the feet form a straight line on the floor, toes facing away from each other; a way of holding the body, developed in ballet, that allows the dancer more articulation, speed, and variety of movement.

TURNS À LA SECONDE Usually performed by the danseur, these are PIROUETTES with one leg extended out to the side, À LA SECONDE.

TUTU Refers to the ballet skirt worn by ballerinas; either romantic, which extends to the ankle or mid-calf; or classical, which juts out from the waist so that the entire leg is visible.

VARIATION A solo, or *pas seul*.

WHITE BALLETS (or *ballets blancs*) Refers to those ballets in which the women wear long white TUTUS, such as *Giselle*, *Les Sylphides*, *La Sylphide*, *Swan Lake*.

WINGS Sections at either side of the stage through which the dancers exit or enter.

WORKING LEG The leg that is delineating movement.

LIST OF

ILLUSTRATIONS

INDEX